KU-245-435

ISEB
Independent Schools
Examinations Board

FRENCH
ISEB Revision Guide

James Savile
Edited by Joyce Čapek

ISEB
Independent Schools
Examinations Board

www.galorepark.co.uk

GALORE PARK

Published by ISEB Publications, an imprint of Galore Park Publications Ltd
19/21 Sayers Lane, Tenterden, Kent TN30 6BW
www.galorepark.co.uk

Text copyright © James Savile 2010

The right of James Savile to be identified as the author of this work has been
asserted by him in accordance with sections 77 and 78 of the Copyright,
Designs and Patents Act 1988.

Design and typesetting by Typetechnique

Printed by Charlesworth Press, Wakefield

ISBN 978 1 907047 619

All rights reserved: no part of this publication may be reproduced, stored in
a retrieval system, or transmitted in any form or by any means, electronic,
mechanical, photocopying, recording or otherwise, without either the prior
written permission of the copyright owner or a licence permitting restricted
copying issued by the Copyright Licensing Agency, Saffron House,
6-10 Kirby Street, London EC1N 8TS.

First published 2012, reprinted September 2012

Details of other ISEB Revision Guides for Common Entrance, examination
papers and Galore Park publications are available at www.galorepark.co.uk

Front cover photo © Chris Howes/Wild Places Photography/Alamy

Illustrations on the following pages by Ian Douglass: p56, p123, p124

The audio material referred to in this book is available as a download from
www.frenchrevisionguide.com

A CD version is also available to purchase from www.galorepark.co.uk
ISBN 978 1 907047 831

About the author

James Savile has taught French for nearly 20 years. He trained as an Independent Schools Inspector, has set French examinations for the Independent Schools Examinations Board and has been Head of Modern Languages in several prep schools. He is a former school governor, a Fellow Member of the College of Teachers and a Fellow of the Chartered Institute of Educational Assessors. In 2012 he was appointed Headmaster of a prep school in Dorset.

Acknowledgements

The author would like to thank Mr Hugh Walkington, Deputy Head of Mount House School, for his help with this book.

Contents

Introduction

About this book

This revision guide has been written for pupils studying French for the Independent Schools Examinations Board (ISEB) Common Entrance examination.

Chapter 1 begins with a description of the four papers that make up the examination: Speaking, Listening, Reading and Writing, with each skill comprising 25% of the exam. Candidates will find it helpful to know the format of each paper and to familiarise themselves with the style of questions they will meet.

Chapter 2 covers all the grammar candidates need to know, and some practice exercises are provided to test your knowledge and understanding. This is followed by a useful chapter on how to approach the writing paper, which is for many candidates the most challenging part of the examination.

Subsequent chapters cover all the Common Entrance topics (see page 5 for the list of CE topics) with sample CE style questions giving candidates practice in the four skills. You will find lots of important vocabulary and useful phrases in each chapter to help you revise. However, these word lists are not exhaustive and we suggest you use the ISEB *French Vocabulary for Key Stage 3 and Common Entrance*, available from Galore Park, in conjunction with this book.

The syllabus

In January 2012 the ISEB issued a new syllabus which introduces two levels in French, Level 1 and Level 2, for first examination in Autumn 2012. This book includes information on the new syllabus (see pages 4–7) and highlights some content which is only applicable to Level 2 candidates with this symbol (at the left-hand side of the page). The grey line indicates where the Level 2 material ends. Please note there are two topics which are only required by Level 2 candidates: 'Understanding tourist information' and 'Pocket money'. Syllabus information and Level 1 specimen papers are available from the ISEB (www.iseb.co.uk).

L2

Revision

As well as looking in detail at the four skills of Speaking, Listening, Reading and Writing, it is important to think about your revision in general.

Get the best out of your brain

- Give your brain plenty of oxygen by exercising. You can revise effectively if you feel fit and well.

- Eat healthy food while you are revising. Your brain works better when you give it good fuel.

- Think positively. Give your brain positive messages so that it will want to study.

- Keep calm. If your brain is stressed it will not operate effectively.

- Take regular breaks during your study time.

- Get enough sleep. Your brain will carry on sorting out what you have revised while you sleep.

Get the most from your revision

- Don't work for hours without a break. Revise for 20–30 minutes then take a five-minute break.

- Do good things in your breaks: listen to your favourite music, eat healthy food, drink some water, do some exercise and juggle. Don't read a book, watch TV or play on the computer; it will conflict with what your brain is trying to learn.

- When you go back to your revision, review what you have just learnt.

- Regularly review the facts you have learnt.

Get motivated

- Set yourself some goals and promise yourself a treat when the exams are over.

- Make the most of all the expertise and talent available to you at school and at home. If you don't understand something ask your teacher to explain.

- Get organised. Find a quiet place to revise and make sure you have all the equipment you need.

- Use year and weekly planners to help you organise your time so that you revise all subjects equally. (Available for download from www.galorepark.co.uk)

- Use topic and subject checklists to help you keep on top of what you are revising. (Available for download from www.galorepark.co.uk)

Know what to expect in the exam

- Use past papers to familiarise yourself with the format of the exam.

- Make sure you understand the language examiners use.

Before the exam

- Have all your equipment and pens ready the night before.

- Make sure you are at your best by getting a good night's sleep before the exam.

- Have a good breakfast in the morning.

- Take some water into the exam if you are allowed.

- Think positively and keep calm.

During the exam

- Have a watch on your desk. Work out how much time you need to allocate to each question and try to stick to it.

- Make sure you read and understand the instructions and rules on the front of the exam paper.

- Allow some time at the start to read and consider the questions carefully before writing anything.

- Read all the questions at least twice. Don't rush into answering before you have a chance to think about it.

- If a question is particularly hard move on to the next one. Go back to it if you have time at the end.

- Leave yourself a little time at the end to check over your work.

Revision techniques

As you are having to cover a lot of vocabulary, here is a list of points to remember when revising:

- Use the LOOK–COVER–WRITE–CHECK technique.

- Always revise words from French into English then from English into French.

- Revise a few words at a time and in short regular intervals over a period of time.

- Start revising well in advance, not at the last minute before a test or examination.

- Connect a picture to a word in your mind to help you remember it.

- Ask someone to test you.

- Remember that, as well as spelling French words correctly, you need to use the proper accents where appropriate.

New syllabus information

The following information is a direct transcript of the latest ISEB French syllabus, which was revised in January 2012 for first examination in Autumn 2012.

Introduction

This syllabus has been devised in accordance with the requirements of the National Curriculum for modern languages and aligns with National Curriculum levels 1–6. In French there are tiered papers: Level 1 and Level 2. Level 1 is aimed at candidates who have studied their respective language for between 30 and 40 hours, or who find languages difficult.

All exercises in the Listening and Reading components can be completed without the use of past tenses and none of the questions will specifically target details in which the use of past tenses is vital. In Level 2 French, exercises in the Speaking and Writing components offer open-ended tasks which allow candidates to show knowledge of a range of tenses, should they choose to use them.

Aims

A course leading to this examination should:

(i)   develop the skills which will enable candidates to understand the written and spoken language and use the language effectively for purposes of practical communication;

(ii)   give candidates opportunities to take part in a broad range of linguistic activities such as those set out in the National Curriculum for modern languages;

(iii)   provide a basis for continuing study of the language and encourage independent learning, including the use of dictionaries, glossaries and ICT;

(iv)   give candidates opportunities to work with authentic language materials;

(v)   encourage interest in the target countries;

(vi)   provide enjoyment and stimulation;

(vii)   encourage positive attitudes towards the use of foreign languages and towards speakers of foreign languages.

Assessment objectives

The examination will test candidates' ability to:

● AO1 show an understanding of the spoken language dealing with a range of familiar topics, and identify and note main points and specific details, including opinions;

● AO2 take part in short conversations, giving and obtaining information and opinions;

- AO3 show an understanding of a number of printed items, ranging from short, simple phrases to longer, more complex texts and identify and note main points and specific details, including opinions;

- AO4 produce pieces of writing, ranging from short phrases to longer passages in which they seek and convey information and opinions.

Syllabus content introduction

(i) The examination is based on the topics set out below. An asterisk denotes a topic which is not required for Level 1.

(ii) The grammar section lists all the material which candidates for the examination should cover (see pages 6 and 7).

Topics

- language of the classroom, including basic ICT
- house, home, daily routine and chores
- life and work at school
- time, dates, numbers and prices
- personal description
- family, friends and pets
- meeting people
- free time activities
- holiday activities
- visiting a café or restaurant
- simple health problems
- description of a town or region
- finding the way and using transport
- understanding tourist information*
- shopping (e.g. for food, clothes, presents)
- pocket money*
- weather

French grammar

(*for recognition only/where appropriate to candidate's ability/senior school requirements)

	Level 1	Level 2

verbs	present tense:
	  (i) regular and common irregular
	  (ii) common reflexive
	  (iii) future tense with aller
	  (iv) conditional: only je voudrais,
	      j'aimerais
	*imperative forms
	infinitive after aller, aimer, détester,
	préférer, vouloir, pouvoir, devoir,
	il faut
	interrogative forms + est-ce que
	
	negative expressions: ne … pas, ne
	… jamais, ne … plus, ne … rien
	idiomatic expressions: e.g. avoir
	chaud/froid/faim/soif/mal,
	faire + weather
		*passé composé with avoir/être
		*imperfect tense

nouns	genders and plurals of common nouns definite and indefinite article partitive article (and de/d' with quantity/negatives)	
adjectives	agreement and position of regular and irregular adjectives comparison possessive demonstrative	superlative
adverbs	*adverbs ending in –ment common adverbs	

	Level 1	Level 2
pronouns	subject personal pronouns, including **on** relative pronoun **qui** reflexive pronouns *disjunctive pronouns: moi, toi, lui, elle, nous, vous, eux, elles	relative pronouns: **que/qu'** direct and indirect object pronouns
prepositions and conjunctions	common prepositions and conjunctions, *depuis	
numerals	cardinal numbers: 0–100 ordinal numbers: 1–10 dates and time: 12-hour and 24-hour clock	cardinal numbers: 101–1000

Useful resources

Study Skills by Elizabeth Holtom, ISBN 9781902984599

French ISEB Revision Guide Audio CD, to accompany this book, ISBN 9781907047831

French Vocabulary for Key Stage 3 and Common Entrance (2nd edn.) by John Ellis and Richard Gordon, ISBN 9780903627467

French Practice Exercises 13+ by Joyce Čapek and Nigel Pearce, ISBN 9780903627788
French Practice Exercises 13+ Answers by Joyce Čapek and Nigel Pearce, available as a download, code D0215088
French Practice Exercises 13+ Audio CD, ISBN 9781905735396

So you really want to learn French, Books 1–3 by Nigel Pearce, ISBNs: 9781902984117; 9781902984513; 9781902984896
So you really want to learn French, Answer Books 1–3 by Nigel Pearce, ISBNs: 9781902984551; 9781902984650; 9781902984902

Galore Park is sole distributor of the Independent Schools Examinations Board (ISEB) past papers for Common Entrance examinations and Common Academic Scholarship Examinations

All this plus much more available from Galore Park: www.galorepark.co.uk

For more information on the Common Entrance syllabus for French and to view Level 1 French specimen papers, please visit the ISEB website – www.iseb.co.uk

Chapter 1: What is in the Common Entrance examination?

The Common Entrance examination is divided into four equal sections (each worth 25%): Speaking, Listening, Reading and Writing. The details of each of these sections are outlined on the following pages. Be aware that the final examinations for the Listening and Speaking sections are a few weeks earlier than the Reading and Writing sections. Your teacher will tell you when they are.

1.1 The Speaking paper

This examination will consist of three sections for Level 2 and two sections for Level 1:

L2
- A role play (*9 marks, for Level 2 candidates only*)

- A discussion on a topic that you have chosen and prepared (*8 marks for Level 2, 13 marks for Level 1*)

- A discussion on a topic that your teacher chooses (*Level 2 candidates*) or that you choose (*Level 1 candidates*) from the following:
  - house, home, daily routine and chores
  - free time and holiday activities
  - life and work at school
  - personal description, family, friends and pets. (*8 marks for Level 2, 12 marks for Level 1*)

L2
Role play

Your teacher will give you a role play and you will be asked to carry out six tasks in French. The paper that your teacher gives you will have English instructions on it.

The role play will be from any area of the syllabus but, as you will see during practice sessions, there are some common phrases that may come up in any situation. If you learn these phrases before your examination, you should do well in the role play. Many pupils find this an easy way to pick up marks. There is a list of these phrases on the next page. Remember that you do not have to translate each task word-for-word. You can adapt the instruction to suit the phrases you know. For example: Ask your friend if he would like to accompany you to the match. You could simply say: 'Tu veux aller au match avec moi?'

One of the instructions will be that you must answer a question that your teacher asks you. Remember that you only have to give a short answer, as long as it is appropriate. If one word is suitable, then that is fine. You are only awarded 1 mark, whether you give a long sentence or a short answer.

A very important thing to think about in your role play is whether you have to use **tu** or **vous**. If your teacher is playing the part of a shopkeeper, teacher, waiter etc., you must address them with **vous**. If they are playing the part of a friend, then you should use **tu**.

Look at the topic chapters (Chapters 4–10) in this book for examples of role plays.

Useful phrases for role plays

This is a list of some of the most common phrases (questions and answers) for many of the role plays. Others are included in the topic chapters. If you learn these you will be well on your way to producing a high quality role play.

Est-ce que ...?	Turns any statement into a question
Est-ce que je dois ...?	Must I ...?
Est-ce que tu aimes ...?	Do you like ...?
Est-ce qu'il y a ...?	Is there ...?/Are there ...?
Est-ce que tu veux ...?	Do you want ...?
Est-ce que je peux ...?	Can I ...?
Puis-je ...?	Can I ...?
Est-ce que tu peux ...?	Can you ...?
Est-ce que tu as ...?	Do you have ...?
Est-ce que vous avez ...?	Do you have ...?
C'est ...?	Is it ...?
C'est combien?	How much is it?
Qu'est-ce que c'est?	What is it?
Qu'est-ce que tu veux?	What do you want?
Combien de ...?	How many ...?
Quand ...?	When ...?
Il y a ...	There is .../There are ...
Je dois ...	I must; I have to ...
Je vais ...	I go/I am going
J'ai ...	I have ...
D'accord	OK

How is the role play marked?

Your teacher will mark the oral examination and each phrase that you give in the role play will be awarded 0, $\frac{1}{2}$ or 1 mark, up to a maximum of 6 marks.

0   Failure to communicate

$\frac{1}{2}$ The task is partly carried out but there is serious error or considerable hesitation

1   Full communication (minor errors which do not affect communication will be allowed)

You will also be awarded a maximum of 3 marks for the quality of your language.

A discussion on a topic that you have chosen

You can choose any topic covered by the syllabus or a topic in connection with a country where the target language is spoken. This may include topics such as a famous artist, somebody from history, a town or region, a celebration or a famous sportsperson. Do not be too ambitious in your choice of topic – a lively account of your holiday in Brittany will probably be more successful than an account of the Napoleonic Wars!

How does the discussion work?

You will introduce your topic and the teacher will ask you some questions. The discussion will last for 1 or 2 minutes. This is a very short amount of time and you need to prove to the examiner just how good you are, so preparation is the key to success.

Tips for a quality discussion

- Once you have chosen your topic, talk to your teacher and involve him/her in the preparation.

- Make sure that the topic is not too obscure, as the vocabulary may be difficult.

- Make sure that your first sentence introduces the topic. A good way to start is to say

  'Je vais vous parler de ...'   'I am going to talk to you about ...'

- Think about the balance of detail so that the discussion is interesting and not tedious. Remember that it is your chance to show off!

- Avoid long lists of vocabulary as this will eat into your time.

- Try to use a range of tenses if you can.

- Practise your presentation and, if possible, record yourself so that you can hear how you come across.

- Do not rush, as this will sound unnatural. Speak at a normal pace, trying not to hesitate.

- When you practise, be aware of the timescale and try to time yourself if possible.

- Think about the type of questions your teacher might ask you and prepare suitable answers.

- Give your opinion whenever possible rather than just narrate. Use phrases such as:

  Je crois que ...   I think that ...

  À mon avis ...   In my opinion ...

- Remember that it is a conversation between you and the teacher but you should always do the majority of the talking.

How is the discussion marked?

You will be marked on the following points:

- How well you put across the information

- The quality of your pronunciation and intonation

- The range of vocabulary you use

- The range of grammar you use

- How accurately and fluently you respond to the teacher

A discussion on a topic that your teacher chooses

L2 Your teacher will advise you about this part of the Speaking paper, the topics that may be discussed and the sort of questions you may be asked. Use the oral questions in this revision guide to prepare yourself for the discussion.

This discussion is marked in the same way as for the topic you have chosen.

Speaking

L1 You will complete two discussions. Each discussion will be on a topic you have chosen (see previous page). The topic chosen for the second discussion must be different to that chosen for the first one.

1.2 The Listening paper

In the Listening paper there will be 25 questions in Level 2, arranged in five or six sections and 20 questions in Level 1, usually arranged in four sections.

This book includes a download of audio material to accompany the listening questions, available from www.frenchrevisionguide.com. You will see this symbol 🎧 next to exercises where an audio track is needed. There is also a CD available to purchase from www.galorepark.co.uk.

Before the examination

Your teacher will prepare you for your examination and, in the process, give you practice exercises. This will help you tune your ear to listening to French. If you want further practice, ask your teacher for more examples which you can use in your free time. Your school may have a French assistant(e) who could help you; this can be very useful as it enables you to hear regional accents.

You may also be able to watch French television or listen to French radio, which you can also access on the internet. You would not be expected to understand it all but it can be good practice to listen out for key words. If you do this, ensure that you have no distractions and that you can concentrate.

You need to practise listening to French without seeing the person who is speaking. If you are listening to the television, turn away from the screen so that you cannot see the person. In lessons you may be allowed to listen to your teacher with your eyes closed for a while.

During the examination

When the examination starts, the voice on the CD will read out the instructions for you. Listen carefully and follow them on the front page of your exam paper where you will find them written down.

You will be given time to read the questions at the start. In Common Entrance, this is two minutes. During this time you can do a lot of preparation. Make sure that you understand all of the questions and know exactly what is expected of you. In your preparation in class you should be made aware of what you have to do in each type of exercise. If any of the questions are in French, go through them so that you understand them before the passage begins. This will allow you to concentrate on the passage rather than worrying about the questions. These will need to be answered in French but not necessarily in full sentences – one word may be enough.

While you and your fellow pupils may not be able to control noises from outside, you can ensure that you do not distract each other during the examination. For example, do not tap your pen lid on the desk and, if you know that you have a cold or a cough, take something to soothe your throat.

Even if you think you have answered the questions after listening only once, you must listen just as carefully the second time through as you may have made a mistake. Do not always jump at the first number that you hear. Sometimes there is a question such as 'How much did Pierre pay for the bag?' and the voice will say that the bags usually cost €20 but Pierre had a reduction of €5. You therefore have to work out that he paid €15.

Remember that you can change your mind but you must make your final answer clear to the examiner. Remember you can take notes at any time so it might be an idea, for example, if you hear a number or a date, to scribble down in French what you hear and work it out later.

All questions have an introduction, which explains in English what you have to do.

Types of questions

Three pictures to choose from

In this type of exercise you have to listen to what is said and decide which picture is most suitable.

- If it is a question about time, be sure to listen carefully to the numbers and the specific time phrases such as 'half past' or 'minutes to'. If you hear the word **moins** it will mean 'minutes to'.
- If it is a question about clothes or appearance, listen carefully for words such as 'long' and 'short' or 'small' and 'big'.
- If it is a question about directions, listen carefully for words such as 'left' (**gauche**), 'right' (**droite**) or 'straight on' (**tout droit**). Make sure that you do not confuse 'right' and 'straight on'. Listen also for 'after' (**après**) and 'before' (**avant**).

Choosing a picture

In this type of question you have to listen to what is said and choose the correct picture. You have eight pictures to choose from and each one can only be used once. In the time before the start of the question, make sure that you are aware of what is in each picture.

Each picture will represent a mini topic such as a room in the house or an area of the school. Ask yourself what words may be used for each one. For example, if it is a picture of a bedroom you should be listening out for the usual words such as 'bed', 'wardrobe', 'table' etc. but also phrases such as 'getting dressed', 'going to bed' and other daily routines.

Multiple-choice phrases

In this type of question you have to listen to what is being said and choose the correct ending out of four possible endings. All four possible endings will have common vocabulary, so you need to work out the difference between them. As in all questions, you need to know what is in the questions *before* you hear the passage.

Gap-filling questions

In this type of question you will be presented with a passage in which some words are missing. Below the passage will be a box in which there will be a number of words. There are normally more words than you need, so do not panic! Look at the words in the box and work out what type of words they are. They could be nouns, verbs, adjectives, adverbs, pronouns, prepositions, articles or conjunctions. In the case of nouns and adjectives, you will need to work out whether they are masculine or feminine and singular or plural. For the verbs, you will need to work out which part of the verb it is, which you can do by looking at the ending.

Other types of questions may include: completing a table or grid; ticking boxes; linking options to speakers or answering questions in English.

At the end of the examination

Always check your answers and make sure that you have written what you think you have written. If, at the end of the examination, you have not been able to answer a question and have therefore left it blank, think about the context and possible answers. If you still are not able to answer the question, have a guess. Never leave a question unanswered as you will automatically receive zero for it. Every mark is 1% of your total. You have two minutes at the end of the Common Entrance examination to check through your answers.

1.3 The Reading paper

The Reading paper for Common Entrance is made up of 25 questions for Level 2, arranged in five or six sections and 20 questions for Level 1, arranged in four sections.

Types of questions

Matching up pictures with phrases

In this type of exercise you need to read five French sentences and decide which picture best matches each one. As in all sections, there will be an example on the examination paper. You may know all of the answers straightaway or you may only know a few. If you do only know a few, look at the sentences that you are not sure about and look for key words that may help you. Take, for example, 'Je mets la table tous les soirs'. This means 'I lay the table every evening'. You may not know the verb but it is obvious that the sentence is something to do with a table.

Reading a passage and choosing one of several pictures

In this type of question you will be asked to read a passage and then some questions. For each question there will be several pictures and one of them will represent the answer. The questions should come in the order of the passage. Be sure to know your question words for this type of exercise. If you do not know which picture is correct, try to use a process of elimination. In other words, you may know that one of the pictures is definitely not correct, so you are then left with just two. Look at the detail in the pictures as this may help you. If you see a picture of a thin man wearing a shirt, trousers and shoes, think about the possible vocabulary that might appear in the passage.

Ticking five correct sentences

In this type of exercise you will see 10 French sentences. You have to decide which five of these sentences are correct by reading a passage.

Connecting a phrase to part of a passage

This type of exercise can present itself in various forms. For example, you may be given a diary extract and have to say when things happened or you may have a few passages with people talking about themselves and then have to write the correct name next to each of a number of phrases.

Gap-filling questions

In this type of question you will be presented with a passage in which some words are missing. Below the passage will be a box in which there will be a number of words. There are normally more words than you need, so do not panic! Before reading the passage, look at the words in the box and work out what type of words they are. They could be nouns, verbs, adjectives, adverbs, pronouns, prepositions, articles or conjunctions. In the case of nouns and adjectives, you will need to work out whether they are masculine or feminine and singular or plural. For the verbs, you will need to work out which part of the verb it is, which you can do by looking at the ending. Then read the passage and you should be able to work out what type of word would fit each blank.

Longer reading passages

Here are some tips for how you should approach a longer reading comprehension:

- Read the instructions carefully.

- Read through the questions before reading the passage as they will give you clues as to what the subject of the passage is.

- Read the passage and work out which paragraph each answer may be in. Remember that all questions should come in a consecutive order.

- Look out for any key words. If you have a question about a journey, ask yourself what type of words might be in the passage.

- Answer as many questions as you can.

- By answering some of the questions you should be able to narrow down where the other answers are in the passage.

- Apply grammatical rules to break down the passage or words. For example:
  - French words ending with -té often end in -ty in English.
  - French adverbs ending with -ment would have -ly at the end in English.

- Never leave any of the questions unanswered. If all else fails, make an intelligent guess. You get nothing for a blank!

1.4 The Writing paper

L2 In the Level 2 paper you will have to do two exercises as detailed below. Chapter 3 provides more detailed information and advice on how to tackle the Level 2 Writing paper.

Question 1
(8 marks)

This exercise requires you to write five simple sentences in French, each one about a picture or a word. You will need to write between five and ten words for each part. Marks will be given for content, accuracy and quality of language.

In order to achieve a very high mark you need to meet all of the requirements with a high level of accuracy and a good range of vocabulary. Use your imagination to create sentences and do not fall into the trap of saying 'I…' all of the time. If there is a man, for example, make him your uncle or father or give him a name. Small details like this make a difference. Be sure of your verbs and, in particular, check their endings.

For example, if there is a picture of a child at the seaside you could write phrases like these:

● J'aime nager dans la mer

● Mon cousin Marc est en vacances à Biarritz

● Quand il fait beau j'adore aller à la plage

Question 2
(17 marks)

This exercise requires you to write a letter of between 80 and 130 words based on some prompts in French. Marks will be given for content, accuracy and quality of language.

L1 In the Level 1 paper there will be three questions, worth 5 marks each, involving gap-filling exercises.

Chapter 2: Grammar section

This chapter sets out all the essential grammar that is required for Common Entrance (a copy of the syllabus is included on pages 4–7). If you have a solid grasp of the grammar, you will be able to speak and write accurate French, which is the key to success in your exam. Remember that every sentence has a verb so it is particularly important to check carefully that you have put each one in the correct tense with the right ending. Learn your grammar and don't be shy of showing off your knowledge when you speak and write French.

2.1 Verbs

Glossary of terms

Verb	A verb is often called a 'doing word'.
Infinitive	The infinitive of a verb is the 'to …' form in English, for example, 'to do'. In a dictionary or word list, French verbs are given in the infinitive form, e.g. jouer = to play.
Tense	The tense of the verb tells you when something happens, e.g. past, present, future.

Every verb in French is always written in the following order:

Singular

Je	I
Tu	You*
Il	He, it (m.)
Elle	She, it (f.)

Plural

Nous	We
Vous	You* (plural, or formal singular and plural)
Ils	They (m., or mixed group)
Elles	They (f.)

*In French there are two words for **you**: tu and vous. Tu is used when addressing one (singular) person who is a member of your family or a friend, or when talking to an animal; vous is used if you are addressing an adult whom you don't know well (e.g. when talking to a shop assistant), or if addressing more than one person or animal (plural).

Verbs in French are either regular or irregular. Regular verbs are divided into three groups: -er verbs, -ir verbs and -re verbs.

The present tense of regular verbs

Note the three ways of translating the French present tense:

je mange = I eat, I am eating, I do eat

'-er' verbs

These are called -er verbs because their *infinitive* ends with -er. To form the present tense of the verb you take off the -er. This leaves you with what is called the 'stem'. Onto this you add the correct ending for each person (je, tu etc.).

je* regard**e**	I watch	nous regard**ons**	we watch
tu regard**es**	you watch	vous regard**ez**	you watch
il regard**e**	he watches	ils regard**ent**	they (m.) watch
elle regard**e**	she watches	elles regard**ent**	they (f.) watch
on** regard**e**	one watches		

*Note that je is written j' if the next word begins with a vowel or h: e.g. j'aime; j'écoute; j'habite.
**Note that the word on means one, but it is often used instead of nous to translate we. It always takes the same verb ending as il/elle: e.g. on aime l'école = we like school.

Some common '-er' verbs:

French	English	French	English
acheter*	to buy	fermer	to close
adorer	to love	habiter	to live
aimer	to like	manger†	to eat
chanter	to sing	marcher	to walk
danser	to dance	montrer	to show
détester	to hate	nager	to swim
donner	to give	porter	to wear
écouter	to listen (to)	préférer††	to prefer
entrer	to enter	regarder	to look at, to watch
espérer**	to hope	travailler	to work

*Beware of the accent in some parts: j'achète, tu achètes, il achète, elle achète, on achète, ils/elles achètent but nous achetons, vous achetez.

**Watch the accent: j'espère, tu espères, il espère, elle espère, on espère, ils/elles espèrent, but nous espérons, vous espérez.

†Note the nous form of this verb: nous mangeons. This is so that it is pronounced with a soft g, not like the g in mango!

††Watch the accents: je préfère, tu préfères, il préfère, elle préfère, on préfère, but nous préférons, vous préférez.

Exercise 1

Put the verb in the correct form of the present tense and then translate the sentence into English. Answers are given at the back of the book.

Example: Je .... dans ma chambre. (danser)
Je *danse* dans ma chambre.
I dance in my bedroom.

(a) J' .... jouer au squash. (aimer)

(b) Tu .... le film ce soir? (regarder)

(c) Il .... dans le jardin. (travailler)

(d) Elle .... un sandwich au jambon. (manger)

(e) Nous .... la robe rose. (préférer)

(f) Vous .... la radio? (écouter)

(g) Ils .... dans la salle de classe. (entrer)

(h) Elles .... dans un bungalow. (habiter)

'-ir' verbs

These are called -ir verbs because their *infinitive* ends with -ir. To form the verb you take off the -ir. This leaves you with the stem. Onto this you add the correct ending for each person.

je fin**is**	I finish	nous fin**issons**	we finish
tu fin**is**	you finish	vous fin**issez**	you finish
il fin**it**	he finishes	ils fin**issent**	they (m.) finish
elle fin**it**	she finishes	elles fin**issent**	they (f.) finish

Some common -ir verbs:

French	English	French	English
choisir	to choose	polir	to polish
maigrir	to lose weight	réussir	to succeed
grossir	to put on weight	punir	to punish

Exercise 2

Put the verb in the correct form of the present tense and then translate the sentence into English. Answers are given at the back of the book.

> **Example:** Je .... une tarte dans la pâtisserie. (choisir)
> Je *choisis* une tarte dans la pâtisserie.
> I am choosing a tart in the cake shop.

(a) Je .... une glace. (choisir)

(b) Tu .... tes devoirs? (finir)

(c) Il .... les élèves méchants. (punir)

(d) Elle .... tout le temps. (réussir)

(e) Nous .... (grossir)

(f) Vous ....? (maigrir)

(g) Ils .... les exercices dans la salle de classe. (finir)

(h) Elles .... de nouveaux vêtements. (choisir)

'-re' verbs

These are called -re verbs because their *infinitive* ends with -re. To form the verb you take off the -re. This leaves you with the stem. Onto this you add the correct ending for each person.

je vend**s**	I sell	nous vend**ons**	we sell
tu vend**s**	you sell	vous vend**ez**	you sell
il vend	he sells	ils vend**ent**	they (m.) sell
elle vend	she sells	elles vend**ent**	they (f.) sell

Notice two things here. First, the 'he' and 'she' forms of the verb have no ending. Second, the plural endings are the same as the -er verbs plural endings.

Some common -re verbs:

French	English	French	English
attendre	to wait (for)	répondre	to reply
descendre	to go down, to get off	tondre	to mow
entendre	to hear		

Exercise 3

Put the verb in the correct form of the present tense and then translate the sentence into English. Answers are given at the back of the book.

> **Example:** J' .... le bus. (attendre)
> J' *attends* le bus.
> I am waiting for the bus.

(a) Je .... la pelouse. (tondre)

(b) Tu .... les enfants? (entendre)

(c) Il .... l'escalier. (descendre)

(d) Elle .... aux questions. (répondre)

(e) Nous .... une réponse à notre message électronique. (attendre)

(f) Vous .... des glaces? (vendre)

(g) Ils .... des légumes au marché. (vendre)

(h) Elles .... de l'autobus devant l'église. (descendre)

Reflexive verbs

A reflexive verb is used when something is happening to the subject. An example is **se laver**, 'to wash (oneself)' or 'to get washed'.

je *me* lave	I wash myself	nous *nous* lavons	we wash ourselves
tu *te* laves	you wash yourself	vous *vous* lavez	you wash yourself
il *se* lave	he washes himself	ils *se* lavent	they (m.) wash themselves
elle *se* lave	she washes herself	elles *se* lavent	they (f.) wash themselves

Some common reflexive verbs:

French	English	French	English
se réveiller	to wake up	se coiffer	to do one's hair
se lever*	to get up	se brosser les dents	to brush one's teeth
se laver	to get washed	se déshabiller	to get undressed
se doucher	to have a shower	se coucher	to go to bed
se raser	to shave	s'entendre avec	to get on with (people)
s'habiller	to get dressed	s'intéresser à	to be interested in
se promener*	to go for a walk	se reposer	to rest

*Watch the accents in these verbs! Je me lève, tu te lèves, il/elle/on se lève, ils/elles se lèvent, but nous nous levons, vous vous levez.

French	English	French	English
s'amuser	to have fun	se sauver	to run away
se dépêcher	to hurry	se trouver	to be (situated)
se balader	to stroll	se demander	to wonder
se disputer	to have an argument	se casser (la jambe)	to break (one's leg)

Note that me, te and se change to m', t', s' when followed by a vowel, e.g. je m'habille, tu t'amuses, ils s'entendent.

Exercise 4

Put the verb in the correct form of the present tense and then translate the sentence into English. Answers are given at the back of the book.

Example: Je .... à vingt-deux heures. (se coucher)
Je *me couche* à vingt-deux heures.
I go to bed at 10 p.m.

(a) Je .... dans ma chambre. (s'habiller)

(b) Tu .... à sept heures trente. (se lever)

(c) Il .... devant un miroir. (se raser)

(d) Elle .... les dents dans la salle de bain. (se brosser)

(e) Nous .... très tôt chaque matin. (se réveiller)

(f) Vous .... à quelle heure? (se réveiller)

(g) Ils .... après le petit déjeuner. (se coiffer)

(h) Elles .... à l'histoire. (s'intéresser)

The present tense of irregular verbs

Irregular verbs are verbs that do not follow the pattern of any of the regular verb groups. The four most common ones are below.

avoir = to have	
j'ai	I have
tu as	you have
il a	he has
elle a	she has
nous avons	we have
vous avez	you have
ils ont	they (m.) have
elles ont	they (f.) have

être = to be	
je suis	I am
tu es	you are
il est	he is
elle est	she is
nous sommes	we are
vous êtes	you are
ils sont	they (m.) are
elles sont	they (f.) are

aller = to go	
je vais	I go
tu vas	you go
il va	he goes
elle va	she goes
nous allons	we go
vous allez	you go
ils vont	they (m.) go
elles vont	they (f.) go

faire = to do/make	
je fais	I do
tu fais	you do
il fait	he does
elle fait	she does
nous faisons	we do
vous faites	you do
ils font	they (m.) do
elles font	they (f.) do

Avoir expressions

The following phrases use **avoir** although in English we use the verb 'to be'.

avoir faim	to be hungry	avoir peur (de)*	to be afraid (of)
avoir soif	to be thirsty	avoir raison	to be right
avoir chaud	to be hot	avoir tort	to be wrong
avoir froid	to be cold	avoir honte	to be ashamed
avoir sommeil	to be sleepy	avoir l'air	to seem
avoir lieu	to take place	avoir envie de*	to want very much
avoir besoin de*	to need		

*Note that **de** may change to **d'** if followed by a vowel.

e.g. **tu as besoin d'une règle**
       you need a ruler

Exercise 5

Translate the following sentences into French. Answers are given at the back of the book.

Examples: I am thirsty.   J'ai soif.
We are hungry.   Nous avons faim.

(a) She is wrong.

(b) Peter is afraid of cows.

(c) You (*singular*) are very hot.

(d) My mother is right.

(e) I need a pen.

The following common verbs are also irregular and need to be learnt:

Remember that **on** takes the same ending as **il** and **elle**: e.g. **on boit** = one drinks, we drink
on peut = one can, we can.

boire = to drink	croire = to believe	courir = to run	devoir = to have to
je bois	je crois	je cours	je dois
tu bois	tu crois	tu cours	tu dois
il boit	il croit	il court	il doit
elle boit	elle croit	elle court	elle doit
nous buvons	nous croyons	nous courons	nous devons
vous buvez	vous croyez	vous courez	vous devez
ils boivent	ils croient	ils courent	ils doivent
elles boivent	elles croient	elles courent	elles doivent

dire = to say	écrire = to write	mettre = to put (on)	lire = to read
je dis	j'écris	je mets	je lis
tu dis	tu écris	tu mets	tu lis
il dit	il écrit	il met	il lit
elle dit	elle écrit	elle met	elle lit
nous disons	nous écrivons	nous mettons	nous lisons
vous dites	vous écrivez	vous mettez	vous lisez
ils disent	ils écrivent	ils mettent	ils lisent
elles disent	elles écrivent	elles mettent	elles lisent

pouvoir = to be able	prendre = to take	sortir = to go out	venir = to come
je peux	je prends	je sors	je viens
tu peux	tu prends	tu sors	tu viens
il peut	il prend	il sort	il vient
elle peut	elle prend	elle sort	elle vient
nous pouvons	nous prenons	nous sortons	nous venons
vous pouvez	vous prenez	vous sortez	vous venez
ils peuvent	ils prennent	ils sortent	ils viennent
elles peuvent	elles prennent	elles sortent	elles viennent

voir = to see	vouloir = to want	ouvrir = to open	dormir = to sleep
je vois	je veux	j'ouvre	je dors
tu vois	tu veux	tu ouvres	tu dors
il voit	il veut	il ouvre	il dort
elle voit	elle veut	elle ouvre	elle dort
nous voyons	nous voulons	nous ouvrons	nous dormons
vous voyez	vous voulez	vous ouvrez	vous dormez
ils voient	ils veulent	ils ouvrent	ils dorment
elles voient	elles veulent	elles ouvrent	elles dorment

partir = to leave
je pars
tu pars
il part
elle part
nous partons
vous partez
ils partent
elles partent

Exercise 6

Put the verb in the correct form of the present tense and then translate the sentence into English. Answers are given at the back of the book.

> **Example:** Je .... mon déjeuner à la cantine. (prendre)
> Je *prends* mon déjeuner à la cantine.
> I have my lunch in the canteen.

(a) Je .... très contente. (être)

(b) Tu .... quel âge? (avoir)

(c) Il .... une chemise bleue. (mettre)

(d) Elle .... la porte. (ouvrir)

(e) Nous .... une lettre à notre oncle. (écrire)

(f) Vous .... quelque chose à boire? (vouloir)

(g) Ils .... au cinéma ce soir. (aller)

(h) Elles .... chez nous à dix-neuf heures. (venir)

Depuis

Depuis means 'since' and is used to describe how long you have been doing something.

Use the present tense (not the perfect as in English) + **depuis** + a time expression. For example:

J'apprends le français depuis deux ans.
I have been learning French for two years.

Je joue au golf depuis trois mois.
I have been playing golf for three months.

The Infinitive

Using the Infinitive

The Infinitive is the part of the verb that means 'to do', e.g. to eat, to play, to leave, to buy.

In French the Infinitive will usually end in -er, -ir, -re or -oir.

e.g. **jouer** (to play), **finir** (to finish), **vendre** (to sell), **boire** (to drink), **avoir** (to have).

The following verbs can all be followed by an infinitive, giving you hundreds of opportunities to write and speak good French:

aimer	to like to	j'aime parler français	I like to speak French
adorer	to love to	il adore voyager	he loves to travel
préférer	to prefer to	nous préférons rester ici	we prefer to stay here
vouloir	to want to	tu veux partir?	do you want to leave?

28

pouvoir	to be able to (can)	on peut visiter le château	one can visit the castle
devoir	to have to (must)	je dois travailler	I have to work

Some other useful phrases that are followed by an infinitive are:

je voudrais	I would like	je voudrais visiter le Canada	I would like to visit Canada
il faut	it is necessary	il faut téléphoner	it is necessary to phone

Note too that in English we say 'I don't like danc**ing**' and 'I hate work**ing**' but you use the Infinitive in French: 'je n'aime pas dans**er**', 'je déteste travaill**er**'.

Exercise 7

Translate the following into French. Answers are given at the back of the book.

(a) I want to go out.

(b) Do you like to play tennis?

(c) We can go to the cinema.

(d) I would like to live in France.

(e) I hate doing the shopping

(f) She must stay at home.

The immediate future

The immediate future is made by using the present tense of the verb **aller** and an infinitive. For example: je **vais nager** (I am going to swim), **nous allons danser** (we are going to dance).

See page 25 if you are unsure of the verb **aller**.

Exercise 8

Translate the following sentences into French. Answers are given at the back of the book.

Example: I am going to draw.
Je vais dessiner.

(a) She is going to arrive this afternoon.

(b) They (*masculine*) are going to play on the computer.

(c) He is going to get dressed.

(d) We are going to choose a book.

(e) Are you (*singular*) going to return next year?

(f) You (*plural*) are going to sing this evening.

(g) Paul is going to dance with Anne.

(h) They (*feminine*) are going to play cards after lunch.

Other uses of the Infinitive

Here are some other uses of the Infinitive (not essential for Common Entrance).

Venir de + infinitive

Used in the present tense, venir de means 'to have just …' etc.

Use the present tense of the verb venir + de + an infinitive. For example: Je viens d'arriver (I have just arrived), nous venons de manger (we have just eaten).

Être en train de + infinitive

Être en train de means 'to be in the process of …', 'to be busy' (doing), 'to be in the middle of' (doing).

Use any tense of the verb être + en train de + an infinitive. For example:

Je suis en train d'écouter la radio.
I am (in the process of) listening to the radio.

J'étais en train de regarder la télévision.
I was (in the process of) watching TV.

Être sur le point de + infinitive

Être sur le point de means 'to be about to …'.

Use any tense of the verb être + sur le point de + an infinitive. For example:

Anna est sur le point d'écrire une carte postale.
Anna is about to write a postcard.

J'étais sur le point de finir mes devoirs quand j'ai vu un autre exercice.
I was about to finish my homework when I saw another exercise.

The Conditional tense

Knowledge of the Conditional tense (translating 'would') is not essential for Common Entrance. However, the following phrases will be useful:

Je voudrais + Infinitive	I would like …
J'aimerais + Infinitive	I would like …
Je devrais + Infinitive	I would have to …/I ought to …/I should …

e.g.	Je voudrais être médecin.	I would like to be a doctor.
	Je devrais faire mes devoirs.	I ought to do my homework.

The Imperative

It is not essential to learn this for Common Entrance but you should be able to recognise it.

The Imperative is the 'command' form of the verb, e.g. 'Come!', 'Go!', 'Wait!'

When you use the Imperative, you need to know whether the person or persons you are addressing require **tu** or **vous**.

The Imperative is simply formed by using the **tu** or **vous** form of the present tense, without **tu** or **vous**:

e.g. **Finis! Finissez!** (Finish!), **Viens! Venez!** (Come!), **Attends! Attendez!** (Wait!)

However, -er verbs drop the -s of the **tu** form:

Mange! Mangez! (Eat!), **Commence! Commencez!** (Begin!)

There is only one exception to the rule about forming imperatives: the verb **être** (to be) which changes to **sois** and **soyez**:

e.g. **Sois sage! Soyez sages!** (Be good!)

The Passé Composé

Talking in French about what has happened in the past is quite straightforward, provided you follow some simple rules.

You need the **Passé Composé** to say what you **did** or what you **have done**, e.g. I ate, I have eaten.

The **Passé Composé** is so called because it is composed of two parts: part of **avoir** or **être** (this is called the auxiliary) and a past participle:

e.g. we watched – **nous avons regardé** (**avons** is the auxiliary and **regardé** is the past participle), I arrived – **Je suis arrivé** (**suis** is the auxiliary and **arrivé** is the past participle).

You will learn in this chapter how to form the past participle of verbs and how to know whether the verb takes **avoir** or **être**.

Verbs using avoir as an auxiliary

For most verbs the auxiliary is the appropriate part of the present tense of the verb **avoir**. To this you add a past participle:

● To form the past participle for -er verbs, change the -er of the infinitive to -é.

● To form the past participle for -ir verbs, change the -ir of the infinitive to -i.

● To form the past participle for -re verbs, change the -re of the infinitive to -u.

Note the auxiliary changes but the past participle does not change:
e.g. J'ai mangé, elle a mangé, il a fini, nous avons fini.

2.1

Exercise 9

Change the verbs from the present tense to the **passé composé** and translate your answer into English. Answers are given at the back of the book.

Example: *Je range* ma chambre.
J'ai rangé ma chambre.   I tidied my room.

(a) *Je finis* mes devoirs.

(b) *J'attends* l'autobus.

(c) *Il joue* aux cartes.

(d) *Elle choisit* de nouvelles chaussures.

(e) *Nous regardons* la télé.

(f) *Vous entendez* le bruit.

(g) *Ils répondent* aux questions.

(h) *Elles écoutent* de la musique.

Verbs that have irregular past participles

The following verbs use **avoir** as their auxiliary but their past participles are irregular:

e.g. j'ai bu, tu as dû, nous avons fait.

Infinitive	Passé composé	English
avoir	J'ai eu	I had/I have had
boire	J'ai bu	I drank
connaître	J'ai connu	I knew (a person)
conduire	J'ai conduit	I drove
courir	J'ai couru	I ran
croire	J'ai cru	I believed
devoir	J'ai dû	I had to
dire	J'ai dit	I said
écrire	J'ai écrit	I wrote
être	J'ai été	I was/I have been
faire	J'ai fait	I did; I made
lire	J'ai lu	I read
mettre	J'ai mis	I put (on)
ouvrir	J'ai ouvert	I opened
pouvoir	J'ai pu	I was able (to)
prendre	J'ai pris	I took
recevoir	J'ai reçu	I received
rire	J'ai ri	I laughed
savoir	J'ai su	I knew

Infinitive	Passé composé	English
suivre	J'ai suivi	I followed
voir	J'ai vu	I saw
vouloir	J'ai voulu	I wanted

Note that we have given the English meanings as 'I drank', 'I saw' etc. but all these verbs can also be translated by 'I have drunk', 'I have seen' etc.

Exercise 10

Translate the following sentences into French. Answers are given at the back of the book.

> **Example:** I opened the door.
>
> J'ai ouvert la porte.

(a) I drank some lemonade.

(b) She drove the car.

(c) He did his homework.

(d) You (*singular*) wrote a letter.

(e) You (*plural*) have read a magazine.

(f) We ran very fast.

(g) They (*masculine*) put the clothes in their bedroom.

(h) They (*feminine*) had an accident.

Verbs using être as an auxiliary

The following verbs use **être** as their auxiliary:

Infinitive	Passé composé	English
aller	Je suis allé	I went
arriver	Je suis arrivé	I arrived
descendre	Je suis descendu	I went down
devenir	Je suis devenu	I became
entrer	Je suis entré	I entered, I went in
monter	Je suis monté	I went up
mourir	Il est mort	He died
naître	Je suis né	I was born
partir	Je suis parti	I left
rentrer	Je suis rentré	I went home
rester	Je suis resté	I stayed
retourner	Je suis retourné	I returned
revenir	Je suis revenu	I came back
sortir	Je suis sorti	I went out
tomber	Je suis tombé	I fell
venir	Je suis venu	I came

Mr Tramp's Red Van

'Mr Tramp's Red Van' is a good mnemonic for remembering the verbs that take **être**:

monter, **r**ester, **t**omber, **r**etourner, **a**ller, **m**ourir, **p**artir, **s**ortir, **r**entrer, **e**ntrer, **d**escendre, **v**enir, **a**rriver, **n**aître.

An important thing to remember when you use the verbs that take **être** is that the past participle is treated like an adjective and has to 'agree' with the noun or pronoun: e.g. **la fille est allée, nous sommes partis, elles sont sorties.**

Exercise 11

Translate the following sentences into French. Answers are given at the back of the book.

Example: I was born in 2001.
Je suis né(e) en 2001.

- (a) I left at 3 o'clock.
- (b) She went out at quarter past six.
- (c) He arrived at the hospital with his parents.
- (d) We went down to the kitchen.
- (e) Did you (*vous*) go to the cinema yesterday evening?
- (f) They (*masculine)* came to the café with their friends.
- (g) They (*feminine)* entered the sitting room.
- (h) You (*tu*) returned home at ten to four.

Exercise 12

Use the chart on page 35 to write the following in French. Answers are given at the back of the book.

- (a) We finished.
- (b) She left.
- (c) We came.
- (d) She played.
- (e) The boys fell.

This chart should help you work out how to select the correct form of verbs in the **Passé Composé**. It may be useful to check that you know all the parts of **avoir** and **être** (see page 25).

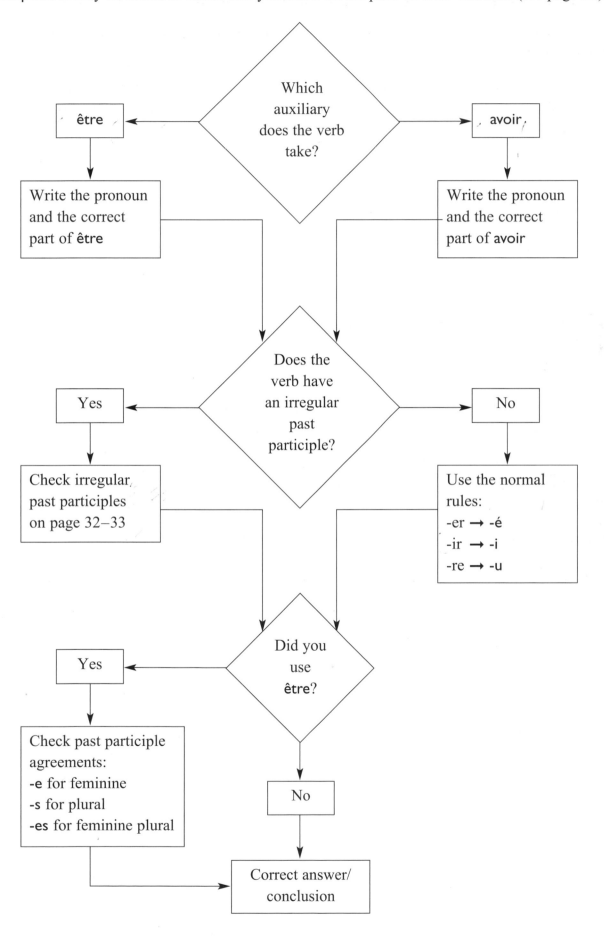

Reflexive verbs in the Passé Composé

Reflexive verbs in the Passé Composé have four sections:

e.g. je me suis lavé = I washed myself.

Reflexive verbs are formed in the same way as the verbs that use être as an auxiliary but they have the reflexive pronoun as well.

Je me suis lavé(e)	I washed myself
Tu t'es lavé(e)	You washed yourself
Il s'est lavé	He washed himself
Elle s'est lavée	She washed herself
Nous nous sommes lavé(e)s	We washed ourselves
Vous vous êtes lavé(e)(s)	You washed yourselves
Ils se sont lavés	They (m.) washed themselves
Elles se sont lavées	They (f.) washed themselves

Beware the irregular reflexive verb s'asseoir (to sit down), which becomes je me suis assis.

Exercise 13

Translate the following sentences into French. Answers are given at the back of the book.

Example: I had a shower at 7 o'clock.
Je me suis douché(e) à sept heures.

(a) She got dressed in her bedroom.

(b) Pierre broke his leg.

(c) He washed in the bathroom.

(d) We went to bed after the film.

(e) They (*feminine*) had an argument.

(f) They (*masculine*) went for a walk in the park.

(g) You (*singular*) got up very early.

(h) You (*plural*) ran away last year.

(i) We sat down under a tree.

The imperfect tense

The imperfect tense translates *was, were* and *used to*. It is used to say what was happening, what used to happen, or for describing what someone or something was like.

Knowledge of the imperfect tense is not essential for Common Entrance. However, the following phrases will be useful:

C'était	It was
C'était amusant	It was fun
Il y avait	There was, there were
Il faisait beau	The weather was fine
Il faisait mauvais	The weather was bad
J'étais content(e)	I was pleased
Il/elle était en vacances	He/she was on holiday

To form the imperfect, use the **nous** form of the present tense of the verb and take off the **-ons** ending. Then add the following endings:

je	-ais	nous	-ions
tu	-ais	vous	-iez
il	-ait	ils	-aient
elle	-ait	elles	-aient

e.g. nous allons → j'allais, nous mangeons → je mangeais, nous faisons → je faisais.

Examples: I was playing the trumpet.
Je jouais de la trompette.
He used to go skiing.
Il faisait du ski.

Être is the only verb which does not follow the rule:

j'étais	I was	nous étions	we were
tu étais	you were	vous étiez	you (pl.) were
il/elle était	he/she was	ils/elles étaient	they were
c'était	it was		

Exercise 14

Translate the following sentences into French. Answers are given at the back of the book.

Example: I was chatting with my friends.
Je bavardais avec mes amis.

(a) He was listening to some music.

(b) We were watching TV.

(c) They (*feminine*) used to work on a farm.

(d) They (*masculine*) used to play cricket.

(e) You (*singular*) were reading a letter in the office.

(f) Were you (*plural*) listening to the radio?

(g) It was cold.

(h) She used to be a teacher.

Interrogative

There are various ways to turn a statement into a question in French, but the following are the easiest:

1. Simply add a question mark to any statement and, if you are speaking, change your intonation.

    e.g. You are going to town.   Tu vas en ville.
         Are you going to town?   Tu vas en ville?

2. Put **Est-ce que** (**Est-ce qu'** before a vowel) in front of the statement:

    e.g. **Est-ce que tu vas en ville?**
         Est-ce qu'il va en ville?

Note that we have listed some useful question phrases in the section on the Speaking paper (see page 10).

Negatives

The most common negative is 'not'; other commonly used negatives are 'never', 'nothing', 'nobody', 'no one' and 'no longer'.

Part A

French	English	French	English
ne ... pas	not	ne ... plus	no longer, not any more
ne ... rien	nothing	ne ... jamais	never

Notes:

1. Ne ... pas, ne ... rien etc. goes around the verb.
    For example: Je *ne* vais *pas*. = I am *not* going.
    Elle *n'*aime *pas* = She does not like
    Notice that **ne** becomes n' in front of a verb beginning with a vowel or 'h'.

2. In the **passé composé** the ne ... pas goes around the auxiliary.
    For example: Elle *n'*a *pas* mangé.
    Je *ne* suis *pas* tombé.

3. With two verbs together the **ne** … **pas** goes around the first verb.
    For example: Je *n'*aime *pas* jouer au netball.
                 Il *ne* veut *pas* danser.

4. Remember that **pas** (along with other negative phrases) is not followed by **un**, **une** or **des**.
    It is only followed by **de** or **d'**.
    For example: Je *n'*ai *pas* <u>de</u> gomme. = I haven't got a rubber.
                 Il *n'*a *plus* <u>d'</u>eau. = He hasn't any more water.

Exercise 15

Translate the following sentences into English. Answers are given at the back of the book.

> **Example:** Je ne joue pas au tennis.
>   I do not play tennis.

(a) Je n'ai rien mangé.

(b) Elle n'est pas contente.

(c) Nous n'avons pas vu les lions.

(d) Il ne boit jamais de limonade.

(e) Nous n'avons plus de bananes.

Here are some more negatives (not essential for Common Entrance). Read the notes below carefully.

Part B

French	English	French	English
ne … personne	nobody, not anyone	ne … que	only
ne … aucun(e)	none, not any	ne … ni … ni …	neither … nor

Notes:

1. These negative words go round the whole verb even in the **passé compose** or when two verbs are together.
    For example: Je *ne* vois *aucun* problème. (I don't see any problem.)
                 Elle *n'*a vu *personne*. (She saw nobody.)
                 Je *ne* vais voir *personne*. (I'm not going to see anyone.)

2. **Personne ne** can start a sentence.
    For example: *Personne ne* sait. (Nobody knows.)
                 *Personne n'*est venu. (Nobody came.)

3.   Ne … que means 'only'. Que comes directly before the word to which it refers.
       For example: Je *ne* vais à l'église *que* le dimanche. (i.e. I don't go to church any day other
                                                                 than Sunday.)
       Je *ne* vais *qu*'à l'église le dimanche. (i.e. I don't go anywhere other than church on Sundays.)

4.   Jamais, rien and personne can be used alone as one-word answers.
       For example: Qui est là? Personne. (Who is there? Nobody.)

Exercise 16

Translate the following sentences into English. Answers are given at the back of the book.

Example: Je n'ai que trois crayons.
              I only have three pencils.

   (a) Nous n'avons vu personne.

   (b) Personne ne comprend le passage.

   (c) Je n'ai vu ni Pierre ni Louise.

   (d) Nous n'allons au cinéma que le samedi soir.

   (e) Il ne va qu'à son café préféré.

2.2 Pronouns

Glossary of terms

Pronoun   This is a word used instead of a noun, e.g. I, me, he, she, it, them.

Subject   The subject can be a noun or a pronoun and is the person or object doing a particular thing.

Object   A direct object is the person, animal or thing that receives an action. An indirect object is when you say 'to me', 'to him' etc:

e.g.

Subject	**Verb**	**Direct object**
I	am eating	cake

Subject	**Verb**	**Indirect object**
He	is speaking	to her

Subject pronouns and object pronouns

Subject		Direct object		Indirect object	
je, j'	I	me, m'	me	me, m'	to me
tu	you	te, t'	you	te, t'	to you
il	he, it	le, l'	him, it	lui	to him
elle	she, it	la, l'	her, it	lui	to her
on	one	—	—	—	—
nous	we	nous	us	nous	to us
vous	you	vous	you	vous	to you
ils	they	les	them	leur	to them
elles	they	les	them	leur	to them

Note that j', m', t', l' are used before a vowel: e.g. j'arrive, je l'ai vu.

Order of object pronouns

All object pronouns go before the verb, or before the auxiliary verb in the **passé composé**.

Je **le** vois	I see **him**
Nous **l'**adorons	We love **him**
Je **lui** ai parlé	I spoke to **him**
Il **m'**a rencontré	He met **me**

Two more useful object pronouns: y and en

The word y means 'there' and it goes in front of the verb like the other object pronouns:

Il va au cinéma demain après-midi?	Is he going to the cinema tomorrow afternoon?
Non, il y va demain matin.	No, he is going *there* tomorrow morning.

The word en means 'of it', 'of them', 'some' or 'any' and replaces a phrase beginning with de, du, de la, de l' or des. For example:

Tu as combien de frères?	How many brothers do you have?
J'en ai trois.	I have three (*of them*).
J'ai mangé des bonbons.	I ate some sweets.
J'en ai mangé.	I ate *some*.

Relative pronouns qui and que

L2   Level 1 candidates are only required to know **qui** (who), whereas Level 2 candidates should be aware of the use of **que** as well.

Qui and **que/qu'** are relative pronouns which translate **who**, **whom**, **which** or **that**.

Who is always translated by **qui**, whereas **whom** is usually translated by **que** (see the examples below). Note however that prepositional phrases such as **for whom**, **with whom**, **without whom** are translated by **pour qui**, **avec qui**, **sans qui**.

When deciding whether to use **qui** or **que**, note that **qui** will normally be directly followed by the verb, whereas **que** will normally be followed by a noun or subject pronoun.

e.g.   Le garçon qui est dans la voiture est mon cousin.
The boy who is in the car is my cousin.

Le livre qui était dans mon sac a disparu.
The book which was in my bag has disappeared.

Le garçon que tu as vu est mon cousin.
The boy whom/that you saw is my cousin.

Le livre que j'ai lu hier soir est bon.
The book which/that I read yesterday evening is good.

Le chien qu'elle préfère est le terrier.
The dog that she prefers is the terrier.

2.3 Nouns

Glossary of terms

Noun	A noun is used to name a person, a place, an object or an abstract quality such as politeness.
Singular	A noun is singular when there is only one of it, e.g. boy, child, car.
Plural	A noun is plural when there are more than one of them, e.g. boys, children, cars.
Gender	All nouns in French are either masculine or feminine. The gender of a word may be different to what might be expected in English.
Article	The definite article in English is 'the'. The indefinite article in English is 'a' or 'an'.

Definite and indefinite articles

English	Masculine singular	Feminine singular	Singular nouns beginning with a vowel or 'h'	All plurals
a, an	un	une	un or une	
the	le	la	l'	les
some	du	de la	de l'	des
of the; from the	du	de la	de l'	des
to the; at the	au	à la	à l'	aux

Nouns in the plural

To make a French noun plural, you usually add -s. e.g. un chien, deux chiens

If the noun ends in -al, change it to -aux.   e.g. un animal, des animaux
If the noun ends in -eau, change it to -eaux.   e.g. un chapeau, des chapeaux

43

Exercise 17

Look at the words below, paying particular attention to whether they are masculine or feminine, then fill in the blanks. Answers are given at the back of the book.

> dog: chien (m.)
> house: maison (f.)
> shop: magasin (m.)
> hotel: hôtel (m.)
> cheese: fromage (m.)
> water: eau (f.)
> apple: pomme (f.)

(a)	a dog	_____ chien
(b)	the house	_____ maison
(c)	some shops	_____ magasins
(d)	some water	_____ eau
(e)	some cheese	_____ fromage
(f)	an apple	_____ pomme
(g)	some apples	_____ pommes
(h)	to the shops	_____ magasins
(i)	to the house	_____ maison
(j)	at the hotel	_____ hôtel
(k)	the name of the dog	le nom _____ chien
(l)	at the shops	_____ magasins

Translating 'some' and 'of'

We have seen that the word 'some' can be translated by du, de la, de l' or des:

e.g. du fromage, de la confiture, de l'eau, des oranges.

If the noun is preceded by a quantity the du, de la, de l' and des change to just de or d' (before a vowel).

For example:

du fromage	BUT	un kilo de fromage (a kilo of cheese)
de la confiture	BUT	un pot de confiture (a jar of jam)
des chocolats	BUT	une boîte de chocolats (a box of chocolates)
de l'eau	BUT	une bouteille d'eau (a bottle of water)
des bonbons	BUT	un paquet de bonbons (a packet of sweets)

The same rule applies after the word **pas**:

For example:

| J'ai des livres. | | Je n'ai pas de livres. |
| I have some books. | BUT | I don't have any books. |

| Avez-vous des croissants? | | Nous n'avons pas de croissants. |
| Do you have some croissants? | BUT | We don't have any croissants. |

Other important uses of 'au', 'du' and 'de la' after 'jouer'

In English we say 'I play football' and 'I play the piano'.

In French we differentiate between sport and musical instruments:

je joue au rugby	je joue du piano
je joue au tennis	je joue du violin
je joue au foot	je joue de la flûte
	je joue de la clarinette

2.4 Adjectives

Glossary of terms

Adjective	An adjective describes a noun. In French, adjectives must agree with the noun that they are describing, that is to say they must be singular or plural, masculine or feminine.
Agreement	Adjectives and some past participles in French change their ending to make them feminine or plural.
Comparative	This is when two or more things are compared; so one thing is said to be 'bigger' or 'faster' or 'more expensive' than another.
Superlative	This is when you are saying that something is the 'biggest' or 'slowest' or 'most expensive' out of a group of things.

The general rules for agreement are:

Masculine singular → No change   Masculine plural → Add **-s**
Feminine singular → Add **-e***   Feminine plural → Add **-es**

*unless the word ends in **e** anyway, e.g. **rouge, jaune, orange**.

e.g. un **grand** garçon, une **grande** fille, trois **grands** garçons, deux **grandes** filles.

The following adjectives do not follow these rules.

Adjectives ending in **-eux** change to **-euse**:

Masculine	Feminine	English
dangereux	dangereuse	dangerous
heureux	heureuse	happy
joyeux	joyeuse	happy/joyful
paresseux	paresseuse	lazy
délicieux	délicieuse	delicious

Adjectives ending in **-f** change to **-ve**:

Masculine	Feminine	English
actif	active	active
neuf	neuve	brand new
sportif	sportive	sporty

Adjectives ending in -n change to -nne:

Masculine	Feminine	English
ancien	ancienne	old
bon	bonne	good

Adjectives ending in -er change to -ère:

Masculine	Feminine	English
premier	première	first

Some adjectives have to be learnt as they do not follow any rules. Here are some common ones:

Masculine	Feminine	English
beau*	belle	beautiful/handsome
blanc	blanche	white
gentil	gentille	kind
gros	grosse	fat
long	longue	long
nouveau*	nouvelle	new
vieux*	vieille	old

*Before a masculine noun beginning with a vowel or h, these change to bel, nouvel, vieil.
For example: un bel homme, un vieil arbre.

The position of adjectives

Most adjectives come *after* the noun they are describing. This includes all the colours: e.g. un chien blanc, des chaussures noires. There are 17 exceptions. The following rhyme will help you remember the adjectives that come *before* the noun that they are describing.

mauvais, méchant, vilain, beau,
petit, haut, vieux, joli, gros,
nouveau, gentil, jeune et bon,
grand, meilleur, vaste et long.

e.g. un petit chien noir; une belle maison blanche.

Some adjectives change their meaning depending on whether they are before the noun or after it.

ancien

un ancien élève	a former pupil
un bâtiment ancien	an ancient building

cher (m.), **chère** (f.)

un cher ami	a dear (male) friend
une chère amie	a dear (female) friend
un chapeau cher	an expensive hat
une chemise chère	an expensive shirt

même

la même chemise	the same shirt
le jour même	the very day

pauvre

pauvre Pierre	poor Pierre
une famille pauvre	a poor family

propre

sa propre chambre	his/her own bedroom
sa robe propre	her clean dress

Look at the following sentences and notice the positions of the adjectives and the gender of each one.

1.   Mon *meilleur* ami a une *grande* voiture *rouge*.

2.   Je suis assez *grosse* car je ne suis pas *sportive* et je suis un peu *paresseuse*.

3.   Le *jeune* homme a les cheveux *courts* et *frisés*.

4.   Ma *nouvelle* amie est *grande* et elle est très *gentille*.

5.   Le *petit* chien *blanc* est *méchant*.

Exercise 18

Fill in the blanks making sure the adjective agrees with the noun. Answers are given at the back of the book.

(a)   a red dress   une robe _____

(b)   a delicious ice-cream   une glace _____

(c)   a good story   une _____ histoire

(d)   a kind lady   une _____ dame

(e)   a little brown mouse   une _____ souris _____

(f)   some intelligent pupils   des élèves _____

(g)   an old house   une _____ maison

48

Exercise 19

Translate the following, making sure you think about whether the adjectives go before or after the noun, as well as thinking about agreements:

(a) a big black horse

(b) a little sister

(c) long hair (*Remember hair is always plural!*)

(d) dear Julie

(e) an expensive T-shirt

(f) a pretty girl

(g) brown shoes

(h) an intelligent teacher

Comparison of adjectives

plus … que	more than
moins … que	less than
aussi … que	as … as

Examples:

Je suis plus intelligent(e) que mon frère.
I am more intelligent than my brother.

Elle est moins grande que moi.
She is not as tall as me.

Elle est aussi grande que son frère.
She is as tall as her brother.

The Superlative

The Superlative form of adjectives translates 'the most …' or 'the …est': e.g. the biggest, the most intelligent.

When using the Superlative you just need to know the gender of the noun you are describing, then add the word '**plus**' and an adjective with an appropriate agreement.

e.g.   Marc is the smallest in the class.
Marie and Claire are the cleverest.
The prettiest girl is called Anne.

Marc est le **plus** petit de la classe.
Marie et Claire sont les **plus** intelligentes.
La **plus** jolie fille s'appelle Anne.

Possessive adjectives

English	Masculine singular	Feminine singular	All plurals
my	mon	ma	mes
your	ton	ta	tes
his, her, its	son	sa	ses
our	notre	notre	nos
your	votre	votre	vos
their	leur	leur	leurs

Note: If a feminine noun begins with a vowel or 'h', you use the masculine form for 'my', 'your' (singular), 'his', 'her', 'its'. For example:

my school	*mon* école
her church, his church	*son* église

Remember: It is the gender of the following noun that is important. It does not matter if you are a boy or a girl!

his mother	sa mère
her mother	sa mère

Exercise 20

Translate the following into French. Answers are given at the back of the book.

Examples:	My brother	Mon frère
	His sister	Sa sœur
	Her sister	Sa sœur
	Their parents	Leurs parents

(a) Our house

(b) Your (*plural*) aunt

(c) His mother

(d) Her cats

(e) Our children

(f) Your (*singular*) bedroom

(g) Their school

(h) My grandmother

Demonstrative – 'this', 'these'

Masculine singular	Masculine singular in front of a vowel or h	Feminine singular	All plurals
ce	cet	cette	ces

Examples:

this house	cette maison
these books	ces livres
this book	ce livre
this man	cet homme

2.5 Adverbs

Glossary of terms

Adverb   An adverb describes how somebody does something.

Formation of adverbs

1. Most adverbs are formed from a corresponding adjective. To form an adverb from the adjective, make the adjective feminine and add -ment at the end. For example:

Masculine adjective	Feminine adjective	Adverb	English for the adverb
doux	douce	doucement	gently
malheureux	malheureuse	malheureusement	unfortunately

A common exception:

Masculine adjective	Feminine adjective	Adverb	English for the adverb
gentil	gentille	gentiment	kindly

2. If the masculine adjective ends in a vowel, add -ment to the masculine form. For example:

    facile = easy   facilement = easily

3. If the masculine adjective ends in -ant, the adverb ends in -ammant. For example:

    constant = constant   constammant = constantly

4. If the masculine adjective ends in -ent, the adverb ends in -emment. For example:

    récent = recent   récemment = recently

    An exception to this is lent (slow) which becomes lentement (slowly).

5. Sometimes the final e of the feminine form of the adjective becomes é. For example:

    énorme (huge)   énormément (hugely)

6. Not all French adverbs are formed in this way. Some just have to be learned:

    beaucoup   a lot
    bien   well
    longtemps   for a long time
    loin   far
    mal   badly
    peu   little, not much
    tard   late
    tôt   early
    vite   quickly

Position of adverbs

Adverbs normally come after the verb. For example:

Il marche lentement.   He walks slowly.

Most adverbs come after the past participle in the **Passé Composé**:

L'homme a conduit dangereusement.   The man drove dangerously.

However, a few common adverbs go between the auxiliary and the past participle.

For example:

J'ai bien dormi.   I slept well.
J'ai mal dormi.   I slept badly.
Il a trop bu.   He drank too much.

2.6 Prepositions

Glossary of terms

Preposition A preposition is a word used to show the relationship between two nouns, for example: 'The cat sat *under* the table'.

Common prepositions:

après	after
avant	before
avec	with
chez	to/at the house of
contre	against
dans	in
depuis	since
derrière	behind
devant	in front of
en	in, by, whilst, made of
entre	between
malgré	in spite of
par	by, through
pendant	during
pour	for
sans	without
sauf	except
sous	under
sur	on
vers	towards
à part	apart from
autour de*	around
à côté de*	next to
en dehors de*	outside of
en face de*	opposite
au milieu de*	in the middle of
près de*	near
à cause de*	because of
loin de*	far from
à gauche de*	on the left of
à droite de*	on the right of

*Note: de may need to change. If the next word is masculine, de changes to du. If the next word is plural, de becomes des; e.g. à côté du mur; près des magasins.

Exercise 21

Translate the following phrases into French. Answers are given at the back of the book.

Examples: near the post office — près de la Poste
next to the cinema — à côté du cinéma

(a) on the left of the butcher's
(b) at Simon's house
(c) behind the market
(d) during the match
(e) opposite the church
(f) under the table
(g) on the chest of drawers
(h) next to the bank
(i) with my friends
(j) in the classroom

It is worth mentioning here disjunctive, or emphatic pronouns, which are the pronouns that follow prepositions, e.g. with me, for you, without him, behind us.

moi	me
toi	you
lui	him
elle	her
nous	us
vous	you
eux	them (m.)
elles	them (f.)

Tu viens *avec moi?*	Are you coming with me?
Voici un cadeau *pour toi.*	Here's a present for you.
Nous allons *avec lui.*	We are going with him.

Exercise 22

Translate the following into French. Answers are given at the back of the book.

(a) without me
(b) for him
(c) behind you
(d) before us
(e) with her
(f) to their house

2.7 Conjunctions

Glossary of terms

Conjunction Conjunctions are linking words words such as 'and' or 'but'.

Conjunctions link sentences together. Common examples are:

ainsi	therefore
alors	so
aussi	also
car	because
donc	so
ensuite	then
et	and
mais	but
parce que/qu'	because
puis	then

Chapter 3: Tackling the Writing paper

As mentioned in Chapter 1, there are two parts to the Level 2 Writing paper:

Question 1   (*8 marks*)

This question will require the writing of five simple sentences in the target language, each based on a visual or written stimulus. Candidates should write five to ten words on each stimulus. Marks will be awarded for content, accuracy and quality of language.

Question 2   (*17 marks*)

This question will require 80–130 words of continuous writing in the form of a letter based on a written stimulus in the target language. Candidates will be expected to demonstrate the full range of their knowledge of the linguistic features contained in the syllabus. Marks will be awarded for content, accuracy and quality of language.

How to succeed in Question 1

To gain a good mark in Question 1 you need to write a simple but very accurate sentence for each picture or written stimulus. You must make sure what you write is relevant to the picture, but you can be quite flexible in your interpretation of it. Let's look at an example:

Maybe you have forgotten how to say 'to play cards' in French. Don't worry!

Look at some of the things you could write:

- J'aime inviter mes amis chez moi.
  I like to invite my friends to my house.

- Hier soir mes amis sont venus chez moi.
  Yesterday evening my friends came round to my house.

- Après avoir dîné, nous avons joué dans le salon.
  After having dinner, we played in the sitting room.

- Voici mon ami Paul, ma soeur Marie et moi.
  This is my friend Paul, my sister Marie and me.

Don't be afraid of simplicity but, if you can, try to vary the tenses you use in your sentences and show different structures. In each of the sentences above you would have impressed your examiner, with an infinitive phrase in the first sentence, a past tense and correct agreement in the second, a past tense and use of **après avoir** in the third, and good use of possessive pronouns in the fourth. In none have we used the phrase **jouer aux cartes**, but now that you know it, here's a fifth example:

- Hier après-midi, j'ai joué aux cartes avec mes amis.
  Yesterday evening I played cards with my friends.

Don't worry if you exceed the recommended 10 words and you write 11 or 12, but avoid going beyond that. The more you write, the more likely you are to make a mistake! On the other hand, if you write only five words for each sentence, you are not giving yourself a real chance to show what you know.

Here is another example:

Here are some possible answers:

- Voici ma mère avec notre chien.
  Here's my mother with our dog.

- Maman aime promener le chien tous les jours.
  Mum likes to walk the dog every day.

- J'aime faire des promenades avec mon chien Bruno.
  I like going for walks with my dog Bruno.

- Hier j'ai fait une promenade au parc.
  Yesterday I went for a walk to the park.

- Quand il fait beau, je promène le chien dans le parc.
  When the weather is fine, I walk the dog in the park.

- Mon chien, qui s'appelle Rufus, est très mignon.
  My dog, who is called Rufus, is very cute.

- Est-ce que tu aimes les chiens?
  Do you like dogs?

- Tu veux promener le chien avec moi?
  Do you want to walk the dog with me?

- Nous avons un grand chien noir et blanc.
  We have a big black and white dog.

Note that there are a couple of questions amongst those sentences. It adds a little bit of interest to your writing. Try to include one in your exam.

How to succeed in Question 2

Here is an example of the type of question you may get in the exam for Question 2:

You are writing to a French friend about a special day. Write between 80 and 130 words.
You must mention at least four of the following points:

- Le départ en bus
- La plage
- Le repas
- Les activités
- Le soir

The key to this kind of exercise is planning.

It is a good idea to ask yourself questions when you read the title. Here is the same question with the points in English with key question words written next to the points.

You are writing to a French friend about a special day. Write between 80 and 130 words.
You must mention at least four of the following points:

The departure by bus	When – date and time? From where? Bus number? Type and cost of ticket? With whom?
The beach	Arrived where and when? Weather? Activities on beach?
The meal	Where (include short description)? Ate? Drank? Cost? Sat where? With whom?
The activities	What? Where? When? Why? With whom? How long? Cost?
The evening	Activities? Where? Cost? With whom? Opinion?

By asking yourself these questions you can form an idea in your head about what you want to write. Once you have this you need to think about how you are going to write the letter.

You may not feel able yet to write about all these things. The following chapters will give you lots of vocabulary and phrases to help you, as well as lots of questions to practise with. You can have a go at writing this letter at the end of Chapter 9.

How to write a letter

3

> Sherborne, le 20 mars
>
> Cher Marc,
>
> Chère Anne,
>
>   *Opening sentence(s)**
>
>   *Answer the questions/do the task as asked*
>
>   *Finishing sentence(s)**
>
>   Amitiés
>
>   *Your name*

Opening sentences

Merci de ta lettre que j'ai reçue hier matin.	Thank you for your letter which I received yesterday morning.
Je suis content(e) de savoir que tu vas bien.	I am pleased to know that you are well.
Ici nous allons tous très bien.	We are all very well here.
Je veux te parler de …	I want to tell you about …

Finishing sentences

En attendant de tes nouvelles.	Waiting to hear your news.
Écris-moi vite.	Write back quickly.
Amitiés/Amicalement	Best regards (literally friendly greetings)
Bises/Bisous	Kisses (Note the French never sign off with xxx)

*The opening and finishing sentences should not be included in your 80–130 word count, but they help to make a good impression.

You now have the ideas and the structure but need to put it all together.

Expanding your sentences

The following ideas should help you expand your sentences to make your writing more interesting. Think beyond the verb! Add details such as WHEN you did something, WHERE, WHO WITH, WHY, HOW YOU WENT THERE, WHAT IT WAS LIKE. Here are a couple of examples of how to expand your writing:

Example A

1. Je suis allé à la plage.
   I went to the beach.

2. Hier après-midi je suis allé à la plage.
   Yesterday afternoon I went to the beach.

3. Hier après-midi je suis allé à la plage avec mes parents.
   Yesterday afternoon I went to the beach with my parents.

4. Hier après-midi il faisait très chaud alors mes parents et moi avons décidé d'aller à la plage.
   Yesterday afternoon it was very hot so my parents and I decided to go to the beach.

5. Hier après-midi, il faisait très chaud, alors, après le déjeuner, mes parents et moi avons décidé d'aller à la plage qui est à dix minutes en bus de notre hôtel. J'ai nagé dans la mer et j'ai fait un château de sable magnifique – c'était super!
   Yesterday afternoon it was very hot, so, after lunch, my parents and I decided to go to the beach, which is ten minutes by bus from our hotel. I swam in the sea and made a fantastic sandcastle – it was great!

Example B

1. J'ai acheté un gâteau.
   I bought a cake.

2. Dimanche j'ai acheté un gâteau pour ma grand-mère.
   On Sunday I bought a cake for my grandmother.

3. Dimanche c'était l'anniversaire de ma grand-mère alors je suis allé à la pâtisserie acheter un gâteau.
   On Sunday it was my grandmother's birthday so I went to the cake shop to buy a cake.

4. Dimanche je suis allé à la pâtisserie acheter un grand gâteau au chocolat pour ma grand-mère car c'était son anniversaire. Cela m'a coûté quinze euros mais c'était délicieux!
   On Sunday I went to the cake shop to buy a big chocolate cake for my grandmother as it was her birthday. It cost me 15 euros but it was delicious!

You should be well on your way to forming a quality piece of writing but you also need to think about the style. Your writing should flow well and sentences should be linked smoothly together.

Below is a list of connecting phrases. Learn them and use some in your letter.

enfin	finally	ce matin vers dix heures	this morning around ten o'clock
aussi vite que possible	as quickly as possible	à deux heures	at two o'clock
aussitôt que possible	as soon as possible	au bout d'un moment	some time later
sans hésiter	without hesitation	peu de temps après	a short time later
sans perdre de temps	without wasting any time	tout de suite après	immediately after
vers midi	towards midday	tout de suite	immediately
après cela	after that	immédiatement	immediately
pendant une heure	for an hour	deux minutes plus tard	two minutes later
un peu plus tard	a little later	à la fin de la journée	at the end of the day
une demi-heure plus tard	half an hour later	vers la fin de la journée	towards the end of the day
à ce moment-là	at that moment	de temps en temps	from time to time
soudain	suddenly	puis	then
malheureusement	unfortunately	heureusement	fortunately
par hasard	by chance	ainsi	therefore
pour commencer	to begin with	après avoir fait cela	after doing that
bon, alors	so, then	je veux aussi mentionner	I would also like to mention
d'abord	at first	malgré ça	despite that
donc	so (in other words/ therefore)		

Topics and useful vocabulary

Chapters 4–10 cover all the Common Entrance topics (see page 5 for the list of CE topics) with sample CE style questions giving candidates practice in the four skills. You will find lots of important vocabulary and useful phrases in each chapter to help you revise. However, these word lists are not exhaustive and we suggest you use the ISEB *French Vocabulary for Key Stage 3 and Common Entrance*, available from Galore Park, in conjunction with this book.

Below is some general vocabulary which will be useful for all the topic areas covered.

Cardinal numbers

0	zéro	13	treize	60	soixante
1	un	14	quatorze	70	soixante-dix
2	deux	15	quinze	71	soixante et onze
3	trois	16	seize	80	quatre-vingts
4	quatre	17	dix-sept	90	quatre-vingt-dix
5	cinq	18	dix-huit	91	quatre-vingt-onze
6	six	19	dix-neuf	100	cent
7	sept	20	vingt	101	cent un
8	huit	21	vingt et un	199	cent quatre-vingt-dix-neuf
9	neuf	22	vingt-deux	200	deux cents
10	dix	30	trente	202	deux cent deux
11	onze	40	quarante	1000	mille
12	douze	50	cinquante	2000	deux mille

Ordinal numbers

1st	premier (m.)	6th	sixième
1st	première (f.)	7th	septième
2nd	deuxième	8th	huitième
3rd	troisième	9th	neuvième
4th	quatrième	10th	dixième
5th	cinquième		

Days

les jours de la semaine	the days of the week
lundi	Monday
mardi	Tuesday
mercredi	Wednesday
jeudi	Thursday
vendredi	Friday
samedi	Saturday
dimanche	Sunday

Months

les mois de l'année	the months of the year
janvier	January
février	February
mars	March
avril	April
mai	May
juin	June
juillet	July
août	August
septembre	September
octobre	October
novembre	November
décembre	December

3

Chapter 4: Family, friends and pets

In this chapter you will revise how to do the following:

1. Greet people in formal and informal situations.
2. Arrange to meet people.
3. Give your personal details.
4. Describe people's appearance and character.
5. Talk about your family.
6. Talk about people's jobs.
7. Talk about pets.
8. Describe clothes.

4.1 Meeting people

People

les gens (m.)	people	le/la camarade	friend
la personne	person	l'ami(e)	friend
trois personnes	three people	le copain	friend (m.)
		la copine	friend (f.)
l'homme	man	le correspondant	penfriend (m.)
la femme	woman, wife	la correspondante	penfriend (f.)
le monsieur	gentleman		
la dame	lady		
un(e) adolescent(e)	teenager		
les ados	teenagers		
l'enfant (m. and f.)	child		

Some useful verbs

rencontrer	to meet
se rencontrer	to meet up with one another
se retrouver	to meet up with one another
s'amuser	to have fun, enjoy oneself
s'entendre avec…	to get on with someone

Useful phrases for greeting people

Bonjour*	Hello, good morning, good afternoon
Bonsoir*	Good evening
Bonne nuit	Good night
Salut	Hi, cheerio
Allô	Hello (only when answering the telephone)
Au revoir	Goodbye
Bonne journée	Have a good day
Bonne soirée	Have a good evening
à bientôt	See you soon

*Note that if you meet a man or lady you will probably just say 'Good morning' or 'Hello', but in French you should say 'Bonjour Monsieur' or 'Bonjour Madame'.

Useful phrases for introductions

Je te présente ma famille	May I introduce my family (informal)
Je vous présente ma famille	May I introduce my family (formal)
Enchanté(e)	Pleased to meet you
Voici mon chien	This is my dog
Comment t'appelles-tu?	What's your name?
Je m'appelle …	I'm called …
Comment s'appelle-t-il/elle?	What's his/her name?
Il/elle s'appelle …	He/she is called …
Comment allez-vous?	How are you? (formal)
Je vais bien merci	I'm well thank you
Ça va?	How are you? (informal)
Ça va	I'm fine
Et toi?	What about you?

Useful phrases for arranging to meet friends

Rendez-vous où?	Where shall we meet?
Rendez-vous au stade	Let's meet at the stadium
Rendez-vous à la piscine	Let's meet at the swimming pool
Rendez-vous devant la gare	Let's meet outside the station
à demain	see you tomorrow
à dimanche	see you on Sunday

Sample questions

Try these sample questions for yourself. Answers are given at the back of the book.

Speaking

Role-play practice

Look at the section on the Speaking paper (pages 9–12) for help with role-plays.

4.1   Your penfriend's family come to visit you. Try to say the following in French:

   (a)   Say hello to your penfriend's parents.

   (b)   Ask them how they are.

   (c)   Tell them that you are well.

   (d)   Say that you would like to introduce your family.

   (e)   Introduce your cat.

4.2   Your friend Julie calls you on your mobile. Try to say the following in French:

   (a)   Say hello.

   (b)   Say you are fine and ask how she is.

   (c)   Your friend asks to meet up so ask where.

   (d)   Disagree and suggest you meet in front of the railway station.

   (e)   Say that you will see her tomorrow.

   (f)   Wish her goodnight.

Relatives

Male relatives

le père	father	le grand-père	grandfather
papa	dad	le frère aîné	the oldest brother
le frère	brother	le frère cadet	the youngest brother
le demi-frère	stepbrother	le frère jumeau	twin brother
le beau-père	stepfather, father-in-law	le neveu	nephew
l'enfant (m.)	child (male)	l'oncle	uncle
le fils	son	le petit-ami	boyfriend
le petit-fils	grandson		

Female relatives

la mère	mother	la grand-mère	grandmother
maman	mum	la soeur aînée	the oldest sister
la soeur	sister	la soeur cadette	the youngest sister
la demi-soeur	stepsister	la soeur jumelle	twin sister
la belle-mère	stepmother, mother-in-law	la nièce	niece
l'enfant (f.)	child (female)	la tante	aunt
la fille	daughter	la petite-amie	girlfriend
la petite-fille	granddaughter		

Plural relatives

les grands-parents	grandparents	les jumeaux	twins
les petits-enfants	grandchildren		

Useful adjectives

âgé	old	marié	married
célibataire	single, unmarried	veuf/veuve	widowed
divorcé	divorced		

Writing practice!

Write six sentences giving the names of members of your family.

Remember to use the words **mon, ma, mes** (my).

> **Example:** Ma tante s'appelle Anne.
> Mes grands-parents s'appellent Marie et Henri.

4.2 Describing people and pets

Character

patient	patient	gentil, gentille	kind
impatient	impatient	drôle	funny
poli	polite	marrant	funny
impoli	impolite, rude	amusant	amusing
inquiet, inquiète	worried, anxious	travailleur, travailleuse	hard-working
sociable	sociable	paresseux, paresseuse	lazy
dynamique	lively	souriant	smiling
sympa	nice, kind	méchant	naughty

Appearance

grand	big, tall	mince	thin
petit	small	joli	pretty
gros, grosse	fat	beau, belle	handsome, beautiful
costaud	well-built	laid	ugly

Useful phrases

Je m'appelle Sophie	I am called Sophie
J'ai treize ans	I am 13 years old
J'ai les cheveux courts/longs	I have short/long hair
J'ai les yeux bleus	I have blue eyes
Je suis de taille moyenne	I am medium height
Je porte des lunettes	I wear glasses
Il/elle est grand(e)	He/she is tall
Il a douze ans	He is 12 years old
Elle a les cheveux blonds/roux/noirs	She has blonde/red/black hair
Il a les cheveux marron*	He has brown hair
Il a une barbe/il est barbu	He has a beard
Il est chauve	He is bald
Elle est rousse	She is red-haired
Elle est brune	She is a brunette
Elle a les tâches de rousseur	She has freckles
Je suis fille unique	I am an only child (girl)
Je suis fils unique	I am an only child (boy)
Je suis l'aîné(e)	I am the eldest
Je suis le cadet/la cadette	I am the youngest
Je suis le benjamin	I am the youngest boy
Ma sœur est plus âgée que moi	My sister is older than me
Mon frère m'énerve	My brother annoys me
Je m'entends bien avec ma sœur	I get on well with my sister

*Note that the word **marron** does not agree with the noun. It never changes.

Personal details

le nom	name	le pays d'origine	country of origin
l'âge (m.)	age	le numéro de téléphone	telephone number
la date de naissance	date of birth	l'adresse mail	email address
le lieu de naissance	place of birth	la carte d'identité	identity card
la nationalité	nationality	le passeport	passport

Reading practice!

Select a suitable answer from the box below for each of the questions on this form:

Nom:

Âge:

Date de naissance:

Lieu de naissance:

Pays d'origine:

Nationalité:

anglais	Le 12 avril 1998	Bristol
Peter Roberts	Angleterre	14 ans

4

Jobs

This list is not exhaustive. Check with your teacher how to describe your parent's job.

le métier	job, profession
acteur (m.), actrice (f.)	actor, actress
agent de police	policeman, policewoman
architecte	architect
avocat	lawyer
chômeur (m.), chômeuse (f.)	unemployed
au chômage	unemployed, out of work
comptable	accountant
conducteur d'autobus	bus driver
dentiste	dentist
directeur (m.)	director, headmaster
directrice (f.)	director, headmistress
employé de banque	bank employee
facteur	postman
femme d'affaires	businesswoman
fermier	farmer
homme d'affaires	businessman
infirmier (m.), infirmière (f.)	nurse
instituteur (m.), institutrice (f.)	primary school teacher
journaliste	journalist
médecin	doctor
ouvrier (m.), ouvrière (f.)	unskilled worker
patron (m.), patronne (f.)	owner, boss
pharmacien (m.), pharmacienne (f.)	chemist
professeur	teacher
retraité(e)	retired
secrétaire	secretary
serveur (m.), serveuse (f.)	waiter, waitress
soldat	soldier
vendeur (m.), vendeuse (f.)	shop assistant

Note that when you describe somebody's job in French you say, for example:
He is doctor – Il est médecin
Don't put un or une before the job.

Examples

Que fait ton père/ta mère comme métier?
What does your father/mother do for a living?

Il est professeur.
He is a teacher.

Je voudrais être agent de police.
I'd like to be a policeman.

Sample speaking passages

Read these passages aloud, then describe yourself in the same way.

Je m'appelle Marc et j'ai treize ans. Je suis assez grand et très fort. J'ai les yeux bleus et les cheveux courts et blonds. J'ai une sœur qui s'appelle Anne et elle a quinze ans. Elle est intelligente mais très paresseuse. Elle n'est pas sportive mais elle adore la musique pop.

Salut! Je m'appelle Marie et j'ai douze ans. J'ai les yeux marron et les cheveux longs et raides. Je suis fille unique mais j'ai trois labradors et deux poissons rouges. Je suis forte en biologie et je veux être dentiste. Tu aimes la télé? Moi j'adore les films.

Je m'appelle Louise et j'habite à Londres, la capitale de l'Angleterre. Il y a cinq personnes dans ma famille: mes deux parents, ma sœur Sophie, mon frère Paul et moi. Sophie et Paul sont jumeaux et ils ont six ans. Moi j'ai douze ans et je suis l'aînée.

4

Sample questions

Try these sample questions for yourself. Suggested answers are given at the back of the book.

Speaking

Oral discussion

4.3 (a) Fais-moi une petite description de toi-même.
Describe yourself.

(b) Décris ta famille.
Describe your family.

(c) As-tu des frères ou des sœurs?
Do you have any brothers and sisters?

(d) Que fait ton père/ta mère comme métier?
What is your father's/mother's job?

(e) As-tu des animaux à la maison?
Do you have any animals at home?

(f) Comment est ton meilleur ami/ta meilleure amie?
What is your best friend like?

Role-play practice

Look at the section on the Speaking paper (pages 9–12) for help with role plays.

4.4 A French boy or girl is visiting your school. Try to say the following in French:

(a) Say hello and introduce yourself.

(b) Say you live with your parents.

(c) Say you are an only child.

(d) Say your father is tall and thin and very sporty.

(e) Say your mother is a dentist.

(f) Ask if the other person has any animals.

Sample questions

Try these sample questions for yourself. Answers are given at the back of the book.

Listening

4.5 Listen to Marc talking about himself and the members of his family and give at least two details for each one.

Person	First detail	Second detail
Marc		
Mother		
Father		
Matthieu		
Luc		
Jean		

4.6 Listen to the man talking about his family and pick the correct answer, as in the example.

Example:

He is called …   Jean-Marc, Jean, Marc

(a) In his family there are …
     people.   three, four, five

(b) He has …   three boys, two girls and a boy, two boys and a girl

(c) His wife has … hair   long curly, short straight, long straight.

(d) He is …   an artist, an actor, a teacher

(e) He leaves home at …   7.30, 7.05, 7.35

Clothes

le blouson	casual jacket
le foulard	scarf (silk)
le gant	glove
le gilet	waistcoat
le jean	jeans
l'imperméable (m.)	raincoat
le jogging	tracksuit
le maillot de bain	swimming costume/trunks
le maillot	sports vest
le manteau	coat
le pantalon	trousers
le pull	jumper
le sweat	sweatshirt
le tricot	wool jumper or cardigan
la chaussure (f.)	shoe
la chaussette (f.)	sock
la chemise	shirt
la cravate	tie
l'écharpe (f.)	scarf
la jupe	skirt
la robe	dress
la sandale	sandal
la veste	jacket

Some useful verbs

porter	to wear
mettre	to put on (clothes)
essayer	to try, try on

Description of clothes

à manches longues/courtes	long-/short-sleeved
long, longue	long
court	short
sale	dirty
propre	clean
trop petit	too small

Colours

rouge	red
noir	black
brun	brown
vert	green
bleu	blue
jaune	yellow
rose	pink
blanc, blanche	white
gris	grey

Writing practice!

Test your memory. Once you have learnt the clothes in French, look around you. Can you write a description of what somebody in the room is wearing? If you are alone in the room, maybe there is a photo that you can describe.

Pets

le chat	cat	le lapin	rabbit
le chaton	kitten	l'oiseau (m.)	bird
le cheval	horse	le perroquet	parrot
le chien	dog	le poisson rouge	goldfish
le chiot	puppy	le serpent	snake
le cochon d'Inde	guinea pig	la perruche	budgie
le hamster	hamster		

Useful phrases

Je m'occupe de mon hamster	I look after my hamster
Je donne à manger au chat	I feed the cat
Je promène le chien	I walk the dog

Try these sample questions for yourself. Answers are given at the back of the book.

Reading

4.7   Read the following passage and answer the questions below.

> Je m'appelle Shrek et je suis le héros d'un film très célèbre. Je suis un grand ogre vert. On dit que je suis laid et que je sens mauvais. J'ai de grands yeux marron mais je suis chauve. J'habite dans un marais avec ma nouvelle femme qui s'appelle Fiona. Elle est une princesse mais aussi une ogresse. Je crois qu'elle est l'ogresse la plus belle du monde. Elle a les cheveux longs et roux et les yeux verts. Elle porte une longue robe verte et, moi, je porte un gilet marron, une chemise sale, des chaussettes marron et des bottes.

Find the French for the following words in the passage:

(a)   hero

(b)   famous

(c)   ugly

(d)   I smell bad

(e)   bald

(f)   my new wife

(g)   a female ogre

(h)   the most beautiful in the world

(i)   a waistcoat

(j)   dirty

4.8   Read the following passage and answer the questions below in English.

> Luc habite dans une ferme avec ses deux parents. Il aime habiter à la campagne parce qu'il joue avec les animaux et il aime surtout apprendre de nouveaux tours à son chien. Il y a toutes sortes d'animaux commes les vaches, les moutons, les poules et les cochons. Il aime tous les animaux sauf un. Dans un champ près de la ferme il y a un cheval qui s'appelle Rex. Il a de grands yeux marron. Luc a peur de Rex parce qu'il chasse tous ceux qui entrent dans le champ.
>
> Un matin, Luc était en retard pour l'école donc il a décidé d'entrer dans le champ car c'est plus rapide. Rex était très loin mais il a vu Luc et il a commencé a courir. Au milieu du champ il y a un poirier et Luc a couru au poirier et y a grimpé.

Les poires étaient mûres et Luc en a donné une à Rex. Rex l'a mangée donc Luc a eu une idée. Il a jeté une poire très loin et Rex est allé trouver la poire et l'a mangée. Luc a sauté de l'arbre et s'est échappé en courant. Il a couru jusqu'à l'école et ça c'était la dernière fois qu'il est entré dans le champ de Rex.

(a) Where does Luc live? (Give two details.)

(b) What does Luc like to do with his dog?

(c) What type of animal is Rex?

(d) Why does Luc not like Rex?

(e) Why did Luc decide to go into Rex's field?

(f) What exactly did Luc climb?

(g) How did Luc escape?

Writing

4.9 Write a sentence of between five and ten words for each picture, as in the example.

Example:

Ma mère joue au tennis tous les soirs en été.

(a)

(b)

77

Test yourself

Before moving on to the next chapter, make sure you can answer the following questions. Answers, where relevant, are given at the back of the book.

1. (a) Greet your French friend.

    (b) Greet your friend's parents.

    (c) Introduce your sister to your French friend.

    (d) Ask your friend how he/she is.

    (e) Ask your friend's mother how she is.

    (f) Arrange to meet friends at the swimming pool.

    (g) Say goodbye, see you on Saturday.

2. Read the sentences below and add either J'ai (I have) or Je suis (I am) to each one.

    (a) .... les cheveux noirs, courts et frisés.

    (b) .... les yeux verts.

    (c) .... très mince.

    (d) .... trois frères.

    (e) .... assez courageux.

    (f) .... grosse et petite.

    (g) .... onze ans.

    (h) .... sympa.

    (i) .... méchant mais poli.

    (j) .... un chien et trois poissons rouges.

3. Write a list of five masculine things to wear and five feminine things to wear. Check the lists for your spellings.

Chapter 5: House, home, daily routine and chores

In this chapter you will revise how to do the following:

1. Explain where you live.
2. Describe where you live.
3. Describe the rooms in your home.
4. Describe your daily routine.
5. Talk about what you do to help at home.

J'habite ...

dans un appartement	in a flat
dans une maison individuelle	in a detached house
dans une maison mitoyenne	in a semi-detached house
dans un pavillon	in a suburban villa
dans une ferme	on a farm
en Angleterre	in England
à Londres	in London

I live ...

Ma maison se trouve ...

dans une ville	in a town, city
dans un village	in a village
à la campagne	in the country
au bord de la mer	at the seaside
dans le Dorset	in Dorset
dans la banlieue	in the suburbs
dans les environs de ...	in the suburbs of ...
au nord/au sud (de)	in/to the north/south (of)
à l'est/à l'ouest (de)	in/to the east/west (of)
sur la côte	on the coast

My house is situated ...

Ma maison est ...

en brique	made of brick
en pierre	made of stone
confortable	comfortable

My house is ...

Chez moi il y a ...

deux étages	two floors
au premier étage	on the first floor
au deuxième étage	on the second floor
le toit	roof
le vestibule	hallway
l'alarme (f.)	burglar alarm
la cheminée	chimney
la porte d'entrée	front door
le salon	sitting room
le séjour	living room
la salle à manger	dining room
la cuisine	kitchen
la buanderie	utility room
la chambre	bedroom
la chambre d'amis	guest room
le bureau	office, desk
la cave	cellar
le grenier	loft, attic
en haut	upstairs
en bas	downstairs

At my home there is/are ...

Dans la cuisine il y a ...

le congélateur	freezer
l'évier (m.)	sink
le four à micro-ondes	microwave oven
le four	oven
le frigo	fridge
le lave-vaisselle	dishwasher
le robinet	tap
la casserole	saucepan
la cuisinière	cooker
la soucoupe	saucer
la tasse	cup
le verre	glass
l'assiette (f.)	plate

In the kitchen there is ...

Dans la buanderie il y a ...

l'aspirateur (m.)	vacuum cleaner
le seau	bucket
la machine à laver	washing machine
le lave-linge	washing machine

In the utility room there is ...

Dans le salon il y a ...

le canapé	sofa
le coussin	cushion
le fauteuil	armchair
le tableau	painting
le vase	vase
le canapé-lit	sofa bed
le lecteur de CD	CD player
la bibliothèque	bookcase
la cheminée	fireplace

In the sitting room there is ...

Dans la salle à manger il y a ...

le buffet	sideboard
la chaise	chair
la table	table

In the dining room there is ...

Dans ma chambre il y a ...

le lit	bed
l'oreiller (m.)	pillow
le réveil	alarm clock
l'ordinateur (m.)	computer
le tiroir	drawer
le chevet	bedside table
la couverture	blanket
la couette	duvet
l'armoire (f.)	wardrobe
l'étagère (f.)	shelf
la commode	chest of drawers
la radio	radio

In my bedroom there is ...

5

Writing practice!

Read this description of a bedroom and write a description of your own bedroom.

Ma chambre est au deuxième étage à côté de la salle de bains. Dans ma chambre il y a un petit lit et à gauche du lit il y a une grande table. Sur la table il y a mon ordinateur et mes devoirs. Mes vêtements sont dans l'armoire car je n'ai pas de commode. J'adore la musique pop et je joue de la guitare électrique qui est à droite de l'armoire. J'ai beaucoup de posters de mes chanteurs préférés et j'ai des étagères pour mes livres et mes photos.

Dans ma chambre ...

Je dors	I sleep
Je lis	I read
Je me repose	I rest
J'écoute de la musique	I listen to music
Je fais mes devoirs	I do my homework

In my bedroom ...

Dans la salle de bains il y a ...

le savon	soap
le dentifrice	toothpaste
le rasoir	razor
la brosse à dents	toothbrush
la serviette	towel

In the bathroom there is ...

Dans le jardin il y a ...

le parterre	flowerbed
le bassin	pond
le potager	vegetable garden
la serre	greenhouse
la pelouse	lawn
la remise	shed
la plante	plant
l'herbe (f.)	grass

In the garden there is ...

Other useful words

chez moi	at my home, to my home
partager	to share
déménager	to move house
en haut	upstairs
en bas	downstairs

Pour aider mes parents ...

Je fais le repassage	I do the ironing
Je fais le ménage	I do the housework
Je fais la lessive	I do the laundry
Je fais la vaisselle	I do the washing-up
Je fais la cuisine	I do the cooking
Je fais du babysitting	I babysit
Je fais le jardinage	I do the gardening
Je fais des courses	I go shopping

To help my parents ...

Pour aider mes parents ...

Je fais mon lit
Je prépare le dîner
Je mets la table
Je débarrasse la table
Je range ma chambre
Je lave la voiture
Je nettoie
Je donne à manger au chat
Je passe l'aspirateur
Je tonds la pelouse
J'essuie la vaisselle
Je ramasse mes vêtements

To help my parents ...

I make my bed
I prepare the evening meal
I lay the table
I clear the table
I tidy my bedroom
I wash the car
I clean
I feed the cat
I vacuum
I mow the lawn
I dry the dishes
I pick up my clothes

Sample speaking passages

Read the following passage aloud then speak about your own home in the same way.

5

J'habite dans une assez grande maison. Elle se trouve dans la banlieue de Portsmouth dans le sud de l'Angleterre. Au rez-de-chaussée il y a un salon, une salle à manger et une grande cuisine et au premier étage il y a ma chambre, la chambre de mes parents et une chambre d'amis. La chambre de mes frères jumeaux est au grenier. J'aime beaucoup ma chambre. Mon lit est très confortable et j'ai un bureau avec un ordinateur. Derrière la maison nous avons un joli jardin. Maman s'occupe des fleurs et Papa tond la pelouse.

Sample questions

Try these sample questions for yourself. Suggested answers are given at the back of the book.

Speaking

Oral discussions

5.1 (a) Comment est ta maison?
What is your house like?

(b) Où se tróuve ta maison?
Where is your house?

(c) Quelles pièces y a-t-il dans ta maison?
What rooms are there in your house?

(d) Qu'est-ce qu'il y a dans ta chambre?
What is there in your bedroom?

(e) Est-ce que ta maison a un jardin? Comment est le jardin?
Does your house have a garden? What is the garden like?

(f) Décris-moi ta maison idéale.
Describe your ideal house.

(g) Qui habite ta maison?
Who lives in your house?

(h) Est-ce que tu aimes ta maison?
Do you like your house?

(i) Comment est-ce que tu t'amuses chez toi?
How do you enjoy yourself at your home?

(j) Qu'est-ce que tu fais pour aider tes parents?
What do you do to help your parents?

Daily routine

Je me réveille	I wake up
Je me lève	I get up
Je me lave	I get washed
Je me lave les cheveux	I wash my hair
Je me douche	I have a shower
Je prends un bain	I have a bath
Je me brosse les dents	I brush my teeth
Je m'habille	I get dressed
Je prends le petit déjeuner	I have breakfast

Daily routine (cont.)

Je quitte la maison	I leave the house
J'arrive à l'école à huit heures	I arrive at school at eight o'clock
Je rentre chez moi	I return home
Je fais mes devoirs	I do my homework
Je me couche	I go to bed
Je m'endors	I go to sleep
Je vais à la messe	I go to church/mass

Useful time phrases

à sept heures	at seven o'clock
à huit heures et quart	at quarter past eight
à dix heures et demie	at half past ten
à cinq heures moins le quart	at quarter to five
à six heures dix	at ten past six
à six heures moins vingt	at twenty to six

Sample questions

Try these sample questions for yourself. Answers are given at the back of the book.

Role-play practice

Look at the section on the Speaking paper (pages 9–12) for help with role plays.

5.2   You are staying with a French penfriend. Try to say the following in French:

   (a)   Say you like your room very much.

   (b)   Say your bedroom in England is very small.

   (c)   Say you live on a farm.

   (d)   Ask your penfriend what time he/she gets up.

   (e)   Ask if you can have a bath.

   (f)   Say that you would like to go to bed.

5.3   You are staying with a French penfriend and are talking to one of their parents. Try to say the following in French:

   (a)   Say that you live in a house.

   (b)   You that you live in the suburbs of London.

   (c)   Say that there are four bedrooms in your house.

   (d)   Say that there is a garden behind your house.

   (e)   Say that you clean the cars.

   (f)   Say that you sometimes babysit.

Writing practice!

(a) Write five sentences about your daily routine on a school day.

(b) Write five sentences about your routine on Sundays.

Sample questions

Try these sample questions for yourself. Answers are given at the back of the book.

Listening

Track 3

5.4   Listen to the following passage and pick the phrases you hear from the list below.

(a) I wake up

(b) I have a bath

(c) I get dressed

(d) I make my bed

(e) I go downstairs

(f) I prepare breakfast

(g) I lay the table

(h) I do the vacuuming

(i) I clear the table

(j) I feed the dog

Reading

5.5   Read the following passage and choose TRUE or FALSE for each sentence on the next page.

> Ma maison est vieille et elle est en brique. Mon ami Marc habite dans une maison à la campagne. Elle est moderne mais très petite. Je préfère ma maison parce que c'est plus grand et il y a un jardin avec beaucoup de fleurs et des arbres. Au rez-de-chaussée il y a quatre pièces: la cuisine, le salon, la salle à manger et le bureau de mon père. Au premier étage, en face de ma chambre, il y a la salle de bains. A gauche de la salle de bains il y a la chambre de mes parents. Mes deux sœurs partagent une chambre au deuxième étage.
>
> Mes parents aiment faire du jardinage et ils ont une grande remise. Il y a plusieurs parterres et un grand potager. Moi, je préfère jouer au foot avec mes amis sur la pelouse.

(a) His house is made of brick.

(b) On the ground floor of his house, there are three rooms.

(c) His bedroom is next to the bathroom.

(d) His sisters have their own bedrooms.

(e) His parents grow fresh vegetables.

(f) He enjoys playing football on the patio.

5.6 Read the following passage from Eric's diary and pick the five correct phrases below.

Le trente mai

Aujourd'hui, c'est mon anniversaire. J'ai treize ans mais mes parents me traitent toujours comme un bébé. J'ai un petit frère qui a deux ans et une sœur qui est plus âgée que moi. Elle est paresseuse et c'est toujours moi qui fais le ménage. Quand je me lève, je dois ranger ma chambre avant de descendre en bas pour préparer le petit déjeuner. Maman est toujours en colère si je laisse mes vêtements par terre. Après avoir mangé, je dois faire la vaisselle mais ma sœur ne fait rien.

Le soir, je fais mes devoirs tout de suite et puis je peux regarder la télé pendant une heure. Quand Papa rentre à la maison, il aide Maman dans la cuisine. Après le dîner, je dois faire la vaisselle encore une fois et Papa essuie la vaisselle. Maman dit toujours que ma sœur ne doit rien faire car elle a beaucoup de devoirs.

Eric

Exemple: C'est son anniversaire.

(a) Il y a quatre personnes dans la famille.

(b) Eric est l'enfant le plus âgé.

(c) Sa sœur est un bébé.

(d) Sa sœur ne fait rien.

(e) Maman est toujours fâchée s'il ne range pas ses vêtements.

(f) Eric doit ramasser ses vêtements.

(g) Sa mère fait la vaisselle.

(h) Eric fait ses devoirs avant le dîner.

(i) Papa aide Eric dans la cuisine après le dîner.

(j) Sa sœur essuie la vaisselle.

Writing

5.7   Write a sentence of between five and ten words for each picture below.

(a)   (b)

5.8   Your penfriend is going to visit you in June. Write a letter of between 80–130 words. You must mention four of the following five points.

- Où tu habites
- Une description de ta maison
- Le jardin
- Ta routine
- Le soir

Test yourself

Before moving on to the next chapter, make sure you can answer the following questions. Answers, where relevant, are given at the back of the book.

1.   Copy and complete with the correct French verb:

(a) J' .... à Londres.

(b) Ma chambre .... en face de la chambre de ma sœur.

(c) Mon frère .... la table.

(d) Je me .... les dents dans la salle de bains.

2.   Copy and complete the grid below with five items that you may find in each of the rooms. Pay particular attention to the gender of the words. Check your answers by looking at the vocabulary lists earlier in the chapter.

Dans la cuisine	Dans le salon	Dans ma chambre

Chapter 6: In town, travel and transport, food and drink

In this chapter you will revise how to do the following:

1. Describe the buildings, shops and main features of a town.
2. Give and understand directions.
3. Hold a conversation in a shop, post office and tourist office.
4. Talk about travel and transport.
5. Order food in a café or restaurant.
6. Talk about meals and the things you like to eat and drink.

6.1 Description of a town, directions and shopping

Main buildings and places in town

l'hôpital	hospital
l'hôtel de ville (m.)	town hall (in a large town)
l'office de tourisme (m.)	tourist office
le centre-ville	town centre
le parking	car park
le stade	stadium
le syndicat d'initiative	tourist office
la cathédrale	cathedral
l'école (f.)	school
l'église (f.)	church
la gare	railway station
la gare routière	bus station
la gendarmerie	police station
la mairie	town hall (in small town or village)
la piscine	swimming pool
la place principale	main square
la station de métro	underground station

Around the town or region

le banc	bench	le piéton	pedestrian
le bâtiment	building	le pont	bridge
le bois	wood	le trottoir	pavement
le bruit	noise	la banlieue	suburbs
le carrefour	crossroads	la circulation	traffic
le champ	field	la queue	queue
l'embouteillage (m.)	traffic jam	la rue	street, road
les feux (m.)	traffic lights	la zone piétonne	pedestrianised area
le jardin public	park	sens interdit	no entry

Around the town or region (cont.)

le panneau	road sign	sens unique	one way
le parc	park	toutes directions	all routes
le passage à niveau	level crossing		

Town adjectives

animé	busy	fermé	closed
calme	quiet	ouvert	open

Directions

allez	go	en face (de …)	opposite
prenez	take	devant	in front of
traversez	cross	derrière	behind
continuez	continue	sur	on
tournez	turn	sous	under
entre	between	juste après	just after

montez	go up/get in/on (car, bus, train)
descendez	go down/get off/out of (bus, train, car)
la première à gauche	the first on the left
la deuxième à droite	the second on the right
tout droit	straight ahead, straight on
à 2 kilomètres d'ici	2 kilometres from here
à 200 mètres du cinéma	200 metres from the cinema

Useful phrases

Où se trouve …?	Where is …?
Où est …?	Where is …?
C'est où?	Where is it?
Pour aller à …?	How does one get to …?
C'est loin d'ici	It is far from here
C'est près d'ici	It is near here

Examples

Excusez-moi, Monsieur, pour aller à la Poste, s'il vous plaît?
Excuse me, Sir, how do I get to the post office, please?

Descendez la rue et prenez la deuxième à gauche.
Go down the street and take the second on the left.

Où se trouve la gare, Madame?
Where is the railway station, Madam?

C'est en face de la mairie.
It's opposite the town hall.

Pour aller au cinéma, s'il vous plaît?
How do I get to the cinema, please?

Prenez le bus numéro trois et descendez à la place principale.
Take the number three bus and get off at the main square.

Types of shops

la boulangerie	baker's
la boucherie	butcher's
l'épicerie	grocer's
la charcuterie	delicatessen
le tabac	tobacconist's (where you can buy postcards and newspapers)
le magasin de jouets	toy shop
le supermarché	supermarket
la confiserie	sweet shop
la crémerie	dairy
la librairie	book shop
la papeterie	stationer's (for stationery, not newspapers)
la pâtisserie	cake shop
la poissonnerie	fishmonger's
l'agent immobilier	estate agent's
le centre commercial	shopping centre
le grand magasin	department store
le kiosque	kiosk (for newspapers or ice cream)
le marchand de fruits et légumes	greengrocer
le pressing	dry cleaner's
l'agence de voyages (f.)	travel agency
l'animalerie (f.)	pet shop
la bijouterie	jeweller's shop
la boutique de cadeaux	gift shop

Shopping

l'argent (m.)	money	le rayon des vêtements	clothes department
l'argent de poche (m.)	pocket money	la cliente (f.)	customer
le client (m.)	customer	la promotion	special offer
le panier	basket	les soldes (f.)	the sales
le rayon fromage	cheese counter	la vitrine	shop window

┌───┐

Useful shopping phrases

Avez-vous …?	Do you have …?
Je voudrais …	I would like …
Et avec ça?	Anything else?
C'est tout merci	That's all thanks
Combien?	How much, how many?
C'est combien?	How much is that?
Ça fait dix euros	That comes to 10 euros
Je n'ai pas de monnaie	I don't have any change
J'ai seulement un billet de cinquante euros	I only have a 50 euro note
Merci beaucoup	Thank you very much

Shopping verbs

dépenser	to spend	passer à la caisse	to go to the checkout
faire la queue	to queue	peser	to weigh
faire du lèche-vitrine	to go window shopping	servir	to serve

At the tourist office

la liste des hôtels	list of hotels
la liste des campings	list of campsites
la carte de la région	map of the area
des renseignements sur	some information about

Useful phrases

Pouvez-vous me donner …?	Can you give me …?
Qu'est-ce qu'il y a à faire?	What is there to do?
Qu'est-ce qu'il y a à voir?	What is there to see?
Qu'est-ce qu'il y a comme distractions?	What is there to do?
La piscine ouvre à quelle heure?	At what time does the swimming pool open?
Le supermarché ferme à quelle heure?	At what time does the supermarket close?

In a bank or post office

le bureau	office	la carte bancaire	bank card
le chèque	cheque	signer	to sign
le colis	parcel	la livre sterling	British pound
le facteur	postman	envoyer	to send
le paquet	package	poster	to post
le timbre	stamp	retirer de l'argent	to withdraw money
la boîte aux lettres	letter box		

Sample questions

Try these sample questions for yourself. Answers are given at the back of the book.

Speaking

Oral discussions

6.1 (a) Qu'est-ce qu'il y a comme distractions près de chez toi?
What is there to do near your home?

(b) Tu aimes faire du shopping?
Do you like shopping?

(c) Où est-ce qu'on achète de la viande/des bonbons/une glace?
Where do you buy meat/sweets/an ice cream?

Role-play practice

Look at the section on the Speaking paper (pages 9–12) for help with role plays.

6.2 You are at a bank. Try to say the following in French:
(a) Say that you would like to change some money.
(b) Say that you have pounds sterling.
(c) Say that you would like 200 euros.
(d) Say that you have your passport.
(e) Ask if the bank is open on Saturdays.
(f) Ask what time the bank opens on Monday.

6.3 You are in town. Try to say the following in French:
(a) Ask where the supermarket is.
(b) Say that it is called Carrefour.
(c) Ask if it is far.
(d) Ask if it is the big building on the right.
(e) Ask if there is a post office nearby.
(f) Ask if there is a letter box nearby.

*Note that 'on Saturday' is just 'samedi', but 'on Saturdays' is 'le samedi'. This applies to all the days of the week of course.

Examples: Qu'est-ce que tu fais dimanche?   What are you doing on Sunday?
Je ne vais pas à l'école le dimanche.   I don't go to school on Sundays.

Track 4

6.4   Listen to these people talking and choose the place where they should go.

    (a)   Tourist office, post office, bank

    (b)   Tourist office, post office, bank

    (c)   Bakery, cake shop, delicatessen

    (d)   Fishmonger, chemist, butcher

    (e)   Church, school, town hall

Track 5

6.5   Listen to the conversation and choose TRUE or FALSE for each sentence below, as in the example.

Exemple: Anne a 13 ans.

TRUE

    (a)   Anne reçoit de l'argent de poche.

    (b)   Anne range la chambre de ses parents.

    (c)   Anne fait le ménage.

    (d)   Papa fait des courses.

    (e)   Anne n'aime pas faire du shopping.

Reading

6.6   Read the sentences below and work out the position of each place in the town.

(a)	**La banque**	(b)	**L'épicerie**	(c)		
La rue						
(d)	**La Poste**	(e)		(f)		(g)

- Le cinéma est en face de l'épicerie.

- La boulangerie se trouve entre le cinéma et la Poste.

- Le supermarché est à côté de la Poste.

- La pharmacie est à côté de la banque mais elle n'est pas à côté de l'épicerie.

- La librairie est en face de la boulangerie.

- La poissonnerie se trouve à côté de l'épicerie.

- La pâtisserie est à côté du cinéma mais elle n'est pas à côté de la Poste.

6.2 Using transport

Types of transport

la voiture	car	la bicyclette	bicycle
l'avion (m.)	plane	le vélomoteur	moped
le bateau	boat	la moto	motorbike
le car	coach	le camion	lorry
le bus	bus	la camionette	van
le vélo	bicycle	le métro	underground

Note that to say 'by car', 'by bike' etc. you generally use **en** if you sit IN it and **à** if you sit ON it.

For example: à **bicyclette** (by bike), **en** car (by coach), **en voiture** (by car), à **pied** (on foot).

At the railway station

le TGV (train à grande vitesse)	high speed train
la consigne	left luggage kiosk
la place	seat
la salle d'attente	waiting room
la voie	track
accès aux quais	access to the platforms
autres directions	other directions
deuxième classe	2nd class
première classe	1st class
direct	direct
la douane	customs
en retard	late
occupé	taken, occupied (of a seat)
acheter un billet	to buy a ticket

Travelling to France

la Manche	the English Channel
traverser	to cross
la traversée	crossing
l'Eurotunnel	the 'Shuttle'
l'Eurostar	Eurostar
le tunnel sous la Manche	the Channel Tunnel
le ferry	ferry
Douvres	Dover

6

Useful phrases

C'est libre?	Is it free? (talking about a seat)
C'est le train pour Paris?	Is this the train for Paris?
Le train est direct?	Is the train direct?
Non, il faut changer à Paris	No, you have to change at Paris
Oui, c'est direct	Yes, it is direct
Le train part à quelle heure?	At what time does the train leave?
Le train arrive à quelle heure?	At what time does the train arrive?
C'est quel quai, s'il vous plaît?	Which platform, please?
Un aller retour	A return ticket
Un billet simple	A single ticket

Sample questions

Try these sample questions for yourself. Answers are given at the back of the book.

Speaking

Oral discussions

6.7 (a) Quel est ton moyen de transport préféré?
What is your favourite type of transport?

(b) Est-ce que tu préfères voyager en bateau ou en avion? Pourquoi?
Do you prefer to travel by boat or by plane? Why?

(c) A ton avis, quelle est le moyen de transport le plus confortable?
In your opinion, what is the most comfortable type of transport?

Role-play practice

Look at the section on the Speaking paper (pages 9–12) for help with role plays.

6.8 You are at the railway station. Try to say the following in French:

(a) Ask for a second class ticket to Paris.

(b) Say no, a return ticket.

(c) Ask at what time the next train leaves.

(d) Ask from which platform the train leaves.

(e) Ask at what time the train arrives in Paris.

(f) Ask if you have to change.

6.9 You are again at the railway station. Try to say the following in French:

(a) Say that you would like to go to Lille tomorrow.

(b) Ask if there is a train at about midday.

(c) Ask if it arrives in Lille before 2 p.m.

(d) Say that it is very fast.

(e) Ask if it is direct.

(f) Ask for a single ticket.

6.10 You are on the telephone to the parent of your French friend. Try to say the following in French:

(a) Say that you are travelling by bus.

(b) Say that the bus is late.

(c) Say that the bus will arrive at 11 a.m.

(d) Say that you will arrive in front of the church.

(e) Say that the ticket costs 10 euros.

(f) Say that you will see him/her soon.

On the road

le chauffeur	driver	le sans-plomb	unleaded petrol
le conducteur	driver	le stationnement	parking
le frein	brake	le super	four-star petrol
le garagiste	garage worker	le véhicule	vehicle
le gazole	diesel	la ceinture de securité	seat belt
le moteur	motor	l'essence (f.)	petrol
le péage	toll	l'huile (f.)	oil
le pneu	tyre	la station service	petrol station
crevé	punctured	faire le plein	to fill up with petrol

Verbs

annuler	to cancel	rater	to miss
arriver	to arrive	réparer	to repair
conduire	to drive	stationner	to park
partir	to leave/depart	tomber en panne	to break down
quitter	to leave		

Sample questions

Try this sample question for yourself. A suggested answer is given at the back of the book.

Writing

6.11 You are on holiday near Paris. Write a letter of 80–130 words to your cousin in Montreal. You should mention four of the following points:

- Ton moyen de transport préféré
- Le voyage en France
- Des amis
- Un incident inattendu
- La ville

6.3 Meals and eating out

Meat

l'agneau (m.)	lamb	le veau	veal
le bœuf	beef	la dinde	turkey
le canard	duck	l'entrecôte (f.)	rib steak
le jambon	ham	le coq au vin	chicken cooked in wine
le lapin	rabbit	le steak-frites	steak and chips
le poulet	chicken		

Seafood

le poisson	fish	la sardine	sardine
le crabe	crab	la truite	trout
le homard	lobster	les fruits de mer (m.)	seafood
le saumon	salmon	les moules (f.)	mussels
le thon	tuna	la bouillabaisse	fish stew
la crevette	prawn		(Mediterranean speciality)

Vegetables

le champignon	mushroom	les petits-pois (m.)	peas
le chou	cabbage	le riz	rice
le chou de Bruxelles	sprout	la courgette	courgette
le chou-fleur	cauliflower	la laitue	lettuce
le concombre	cucumber	la pomme de terre	potato
le maïs	sweetcorn	les pommes de terre	potatoes
l'oignon (m.)	onion	la tomate	tomato

Fruit

l'abricot (m.)	apricot	la cerise	cherry
l'ananas (m.)	pineapple	la framboise	raspberry
le citron	lemon	la pêche	peach
le melon	melon	la poire	pear
la banane	banana	la prune	plum

Snacks and treats

un sandwich au jambon	a ham sandwich
un sandwich au fromage	a cheese sandwich
un croque-monsieur	a toasted cheese and ham sandwich
un croque-madame	a croque-monsieur with egg on top
des chips (m.)	crisps

Snacks and treats (cont.)

le gâteau	cake
le gâteau au chocolat	chocolate cake
le gâteau d'anniversaire	birthday cake

Drinks

la boisson	drink	le lait	milk
l'apéritif (m.)	drink before a meal	le thé citron	lemon tea
le café crème	coffee with cream	le thé au lait	tea with milk
le café au lait	white coffee	le thé nature	tea without milk
le champagne	champagne	le vin blanc	white wine
le chocolat chaud	hot chocolate	le vin rouge	red wine
le chocolat froid	cold chocolate	l'eau (f.)	water
le cidre	cider	la limonade	lemonade
le jus de fruit	fruit juice		

Expressions of quantity

beaucoup de	a lot of	un pot de	a pot of, a jar of
plusieurs	several	un verre de	a glass of
quelques	a few	une bouteille de	a bottle of
un bol de	a bowl of	une cuillère de	a teaspoon of
un demi-kilo de	a half kilo of	une douzaine de	a dozen of
un demi-litre de	a half litre of	une portion de	a portion of
cent grammes de	100 grams of	une tasse de	a cup of
un morceau de	a piece of	une tranche de	a slice of
un peu de	a little of		

Note: **de** only changes if it is followed by a noun beginning with a vowel or silent **h** when it becomes **d'**.

Writing practice!

From the vocabulary lists in this chapter, choose suitable items of food or drink to fill in the blanks:

Example: un verre de limonade

(a) un pot de ....
(b) un kilo de ......
(c) une tasse de ....
(d) une bouteille de ....
(e) une portion de ....
(f) un morceau de ....

In the café/restaurant

le menu à prix fixe	fixed price meal	la carte	the menu
le pourboire	tip	la nappe	tablecloth

Meals

le repas	meal	le souper	supper
le petit déjeuner	breakfast	l'entrée (f.)	starter
le déjeuner	lunch	le plat principal	main course
le goûter	afternoon tea	le dessert	dessert
le dîner	dinner	Bon appétit!	Enjoy your meal!

English breakfast

le bacon	bacon	le yaourt	yoghurt
l'œuf à la coque (m.)	boiled egg	la baguette	French stick
l'œuf sur le plat (m.)	fried egg	la confiture	jam
le pain	bread	la confiture d'oranges	marmalade
le pain perdu	French toast	la gaufre	waffle
le petit déjeuner anglais	English breakfast	les céréales (f.)	cereal
le porridge	porridge	les œufs brouillés	scrambled eggs
le toast	toast		

Starters

le pâté	paté	la soupe	soup
le potage	soup	les escargots (m.)	snails

Cheese and desserts

le fromage	cheese
le fromage de chèvre	goat's cheese
la tarte aux pommes	apple tart
la tarte aux fraises	strawberry tart
la glace à la fraise	strawberry ice cream
la glace à la vanille	vanilla ice cream
la glace au chocolat	chocolate ice cream
la mousse au chocolat	chocolate mousse

6

Useful phrases

J'ai faim	I'm hungry
J'ai soif	I'm thirsty
Qu'est-ce que tu prends comme plat?	What are you having as a main course?
Qu'est-ce que tu prends comme dessert?	What are you having for dessert?
Qu'est-ce qu'il y a comme boisson?	What is there to drink?
Je prends …	I'll have, I'm having … (food/drink)

Writing practice!

You are in charge of all the meals today! Write three lists of what you will have for breakfast, lunch (three courses) and dinner (three courses). Don't forget to add drinks.

Sample questions

Try these sample questions for yourself. Answers are given at the back of the book.

Speaking

Oral discussions

6.12 (a) À quelle heure est-ce que tu prends le petit déjeuner?
At what time do you eat breakfast?

(b) Quel est ton fruit préféré?
What is your favourite fruit?

(c) Quelle est ta viande préférée?
What is your favourite meat?

(d) Qu'est-ce que tu aimes manger comme sandwich?
What type of sandwich do you like to eat?

(e) Qu'est-ce que tu aimes boire avec ton déjeuner?
What do you like to drink with your lunch?

Role-play practice

Look at the section on the Speaking paper (pages 9–12) for help with role plays.

6.13 You are in a café. Try to say the following in French:

(a) Say that you would like to sit near the window.

(b) Order some drinks.

(c) Order a starter.

(d) Order chicken and chips.

(e) Ask what they have for dessert.

(f) Order two vanilla ice creams.

6.14 You are in a restaurant. Try to say the following in French:

(a) Ask for a table for five people.

(b) Say not near the door.

(c) Say that the table is dirty.

(d) Say that your parents would like a bottle of red wine.

(e) Say that you would like a glass of lemonade.

(f) Say that you do not have a serviette.

6

Reading

6.15 Read these menus and answer the question on the following page.

Le Bosquet

Entrée au choix
Soupe à l'oignon
Salade au chèvre chaud
Escargots de Bourgogne

Plat au choix
Confit de canard, purée
Faux filet au poivre
Saumon, légumes

Dessert
Tarte Tatin aux pommes
Glaces et sorbets chantilly

Chez Pierre

Entrée au choix
Carpaccio de Boeuf
Soufflé au Fromage
Terrine Rustique

Plat au choix
Terrine de Saumon aux Epinards – Riz Spécial
Fricassée de Mer et sa Julienne de légumes

Dessert
Poire Belle-Hélène
Mousse au Chocolat

Le Petit Lapin

Entrée au choix
Avocat et Oeufs à la Mousse de Crabe
Quiche Lorraine

Plat au choix
Côte de Veau Flambée à la Crème
Steak – frites – salade

Dessert
Crème caramel
Gratin de fruits rouges

Look at the three menus, then copy and complete the grid below by putting a tick to show where you would choose each type of food.

	Le Bosquet	Chez Pierre	Le Petit Lapin
Chips			
Duck			
Rice			
Egg			
Goat's cheese			
Apple			

Writing

6.16 Write a sentence of between five and ten words for each picture below.

(a)   (b)   (c)

6.17 Write a letter of 80–130 words to your penfriend describing a recent day out in another town.
You must mention four of the five following points.

- Le petit déjeuner chez toi
- Le voyage
- La ville
- Un repas au restaurant
- Le retour à la maison

Test yourself

Before moving on to the next chapter, make sure you can answer the following questions. Answers, where relevant, are provided at the back of the book.

1.   Look at the following signs and try to match them with the descriptions below.

Can you find these signs?

1. Antiques	2. Bakery	3. Beware of the dog (x2)
4. Cake shop	5. 24 hours	6. Danger of death (x2)
7. Exit	8. Fires forbidden	9. Kitchen
10. Stop	11. Toilets (x2)	12. Veterinary surgeon

2. Suggest, in French, a mode of transport for:

   (a) going to the shops in your village or town

   (b) going to school five miles away

   (c) crossing the English Channel

   (d) visiting Paris

   (e) visiting the USA

3. Write down the French for 10 drinks and then check the vocabulary lists. Make sure that you include **le**, **la** or **l'**.

4. How many expressions of quantity can you name in 30 seconds? Time yourself and check the list.

6

Chapter 7: Free time

In this chapter you will revise how to do the following:

1. Describe both indoor and outdoor activities.
2. Talk about your hobbies and interests.
3. Discuss TV programmes and give your preferences.
4. Talk about music and give your preferences.
5. Describe what you read.
6. Talk about the cinema and films you have seen.

Likes and dislikes

J'aime	I like	Je préfère	I prefer
J'aime surtout	I especially like	Je n'aime pas	I do not like
J'adore	I love		

Indoor sports and activities

jouer au badminton	to play badminton	faire de la danse	to go dancing
jouer au ping-pong	to play table tennis	faire de la gymnastique	to do gymnastics
jouer au squash	to play squash	faire du patin	to go skating

bavarder avec des amis	to chat with friends
bricoler	to do DIY
coudre	to sew
cuisiner	to cook
danser	to dance
dessiner	to draw
écouter mon lecteur MP3	to listen to my MP3 player
faire de la photographie	to do photography
jouer aux échecs	to play chess
jouer sur l'ordinateur	to play on the computer
peindre	to paint
regarder la télévision	to watch television

Outdoor sports and activities

jouer au basket	to play basketball
jouer au cricket	to play cricket
jouer au netball	to play netball
aller à la pêche	to go fishing
faire de l'alpinisme	to go climbing
faire de l'athlétisme	to do athletics
faire de la natation	to go swimming
faire du cross	to do cross-country running
faire du cheval	to go horse-riding

faire de l'équitation		to go horse-riding	
faire du sport		to play sport	
faire du VTT		to go mountain biking	
faire de la voile		to go sailing	
faire une promenade		to go for a walk	
faire une randonnée		to go on a hike	
promener le chien		to walk the dog	

General sport vocabulary

le ballon	ball	le match	match
le champion	champion	le spectateur	spectator
le concours	competition	l'équipe (f.)	team
le joueur	player		
attraper	to catch		
courir	to run		
participer (à)	to participate (in)		

Examples

Le sport ne m'intéresse pas.
Sport does not interest me.

Le netball m'intéresse beaucoup.
Netball interests me a lot.

Je passe tout mon temps libre à … (infinitive)
I spend all of my free time …

7

Music

chanter	to sing	jouer du saxophone	to play the saxophone
chanter dans une chorale	to sing in a choir	jouer de la flûte	to play the flute
jouer du clavier	to play the keyboard	jouer de la flute à bec	to play the recorder
jouer du piano	to play the piano	jouer de la guitare	to play the guitar
jouer du violon	to play the violin	jouer de la trompette	to play the trumpet
jouer du violoncelle	to play the cello	jouer de la batterie	to play the drums

Reading

l'auteur (m.)	author	le titre	title
l'écrivain (m.)	author	l'autobiographie (f.)	autobiography
le journal	newspaper	l'histoire (f.)	story
le magazine	magazine	la BD (bande dessinée)	comic, comic strip
le roman d'amour	romantic novel	la lecture	reading
le roman policier	detective novel	lire	to read

How often?

tous les jours	every day
le mercredi	on Wednesdays
le weekend	at the weekend
en semaine	during the week
pendant les vacances	during/in the holidays

Useful phrases

C'est génial	It's fantastic
C'est marrant	It's funny
C'est pénible	It's dreadful
Mon chanteur préféré est …	My favourite male singer is …
Ma chanteuse préférée est …	My favourite female singer is …
Ma chanson préférée est …	My favourite song is …
Mon groupe préféré est …	My favourite group is …
Il s'agit de …	It is about …
Ça se passe …	It takes place …
C'est l'histoire de …	It's the story of …

Sample speaking passages

Read the following passages aloud, then try to say a few things about your own hobbies and free time interests.

> Salut! Je m'appelle Tom et je suis très sportif. J'adore jouer au rugby et j'en fais quatre fois par semaine. Il y a un match tous les mercredis après-midi et la semaine dernière nous avons gagné. Pendant les vacances je fais du VTT avec mes amis à la campagne et j'adore ça surtout quand il pleut.

> Je m'appelle Annette et je déteste le sport. Je préfère la lecture et j'aime surtout lire les romans. De temps en temps je lis un magazine mais en ce moment je lis un roman d'amour. Il s'agit d'un soldat allemand qui aime une belle fille et ça s'est passé en France en 1942.

> Bonjour, je m'appelle Juan et je suis espagnol mais j'habite en Angleterre. Tu joues d'un instrument de musique? Moi, je joue de la trompette depuis trois ans et j'adore le jazz. Il y a un orchestre à mon école mais normalement on joue de la musique classique qui ne m'intéresse pas.

> As-tu vu le western hier soir à la télé? Moi, je crois que les cowboys sont amusants. Je regarde la télé tous les soirs sauf le dimanche quand je vais dîner chez mes grands-parents.

Sample questions

Try these sample questions for yourself. Suggested answers are given at the back of the book.

Speaking

Oral discussions

7.1 (a) Qu'est-ce que tu fais quand tu es libre?
        What do you do in your free time?

     (b) Quel sports pratiques-tu?
        Which sports do you do?

     (c) Quel est ton sport préféré?
        What is your favourite sport?

     (d) Quel genre de musique est-ce que tu préfères et pourquoi?
        What type of music do you prefer and why?

     (e) Tu joues d'un instrument de musique?
        Do you play a musical instrument?

     (f) Tu vas souvent au cinéma?
        Do you often go to the cinema?

     (g) Qu'est-ce que tu aimes faire avec tes copains?
        What do you like to do with your friends?

     (h) Qu'est-ce que tu vas faire le weekend prochain?
        What are you going to do next weekend?

     (i) Qu'est-ce que tu aimes faire à la maison?
        What do you like to do at home?

     (j) Qu'est-ce que tu as fait dimanche dernier?
        What did you do last Sunday?

     (k) Comment est ton weekend idéal?
        What is your ideal weekend like?

7

Television and cinema

l'acteur (m.)	actor
l'actrice (f.)	actress
le dessin animé	cartoon film
le documentaire	documentary
le feuilleton	soap opera
le film comique	comedy film
le film d'aventures	adventure film
le film d'amour	romantic film
le film d'horreur	horror film
le film de science-fiction	science fiction film
le film policier	detective film
le polar	detective film
le western	western
l'écran (m.)	screen
la chaîne (de télévision)	TV channel
l'émission de sport (f.)	sports programme
les informations (f.)	news
les actualités (f.)	news
la comédie	comedy
la série	series
la séance	performance, showing (of film)
la vedette	star (of stage or film)
avec Gérard Depardieu	starring Gérard Depardieu

Examples

Je regarde la télé tous les jours.
I watch TV every day.

Mon émission préférée, c'est Les Simpson.
My favourite programme is The Simpsons.

Sample questions

Try these sample questions for yourself. Answers are given at the back of the book.

Speaking

Role-play practice

Look at the section on the Speaking paper (pages 9–12) for help with role plays.

7.2   You are phoning a friend. Try to say the following in French:

    (a)   Ask if they want to go to the cinema.

    (b)   Say that there is an adventure film at 3 p.m.

    (c)   Give the name of the star.

    (d)   Say that you will meet in front of the cinema.

    (e)   Say that you will meet at 2.30 p.m.

    (f)   Suggest going to town afterwards.

Listening

7.3   Listen to this telephone conversation and answer the questions below in English.

    (a)   When does Marc suggest going to the cinema?

    (b)   Why does Anne not want to go? (2 reasons)

    (c)   Where do they decide to go next week?

    (d)   Where will they meet?

    (e)   Why will they meet here?

    (f)   At what time will they meet?

7

Reading

7.4 Read the following interview and answer the questions below.

Q *Salut, Jean-Marc. Est-ce que tu regardes souvent la télé?*

A Je regarde la télé de temps en temps mais je suis très occupé et je n'ai pas beaucoup de temps libre.

Q *Est-ce que tu as regardé la télé hier soir?*

A Oui. Je n'avais rien à faire hier soir donc j'ai regardé le film *Maman, j'ai raté l'avion* avec ma femme Hélène. Elle aime bien les comédies et c'était très amusant.

Q *Est-ce que tu aimes aller au cinéma?*

A Non, je ne vais jamais au cinéma car il y a trop de monde. Je préfère rester chez moi avec ma famille et mes chiens. D'ailleurs je déteste le popcorn!

Q *Quelle sorte de film est-ce que tu préfères?*

A J'aime bien les comédies comme Hélène mais je préfère les films d'action.

Q *Comment s'appelle ton acteur préféré ou ton actrice préférée?*

A J'adore les films de Gérard Depardieu.

Q *Est-ce que tu as vu les films de Harry Potter?*

A J'ai vu le premier film avec mon fils et j'ai trouvé que c'était amusant mais je me suis endormi pendant le deuxième. Je n'ai pas lu les livres.

Q *Qu'est-ce que ton fils a pensé du film?*

A Patrick a adoré le film et il a lu tous les livres. Il veut être magicien!

Q *Quel est ton film préféré?*

A J'adore *Cyrano de Bergerac*. C'est au sujet d'un homme qui s'appelle Cyrano. Il est laid mais il espère pouvoir un jour séduire son amour de toujours, la belle Roxane, sa cousine. Je l'adore car c'est un film de Gérard Depardieu et c'est une histoire d'amour. Hélène dit que je suis très romantique!

(a) How often does Jean-Marc watch television? *Time to Time*

(b) What did he watch on television last night? *Home alone*

(c) Why does he not like to go to the cinema? (2 reasons) *crowded and does not like popcorn*

(d) What type of film does he prefer? *Come Action*

(e) Who is his favourite actor? *

(f) What happened to him during the second Harry Potter film? *He fell asleep*

(g) What does his son want to be? *magician*

(h) How is Cyrano described? *he is a man who is ugly*

(i) What does Jean-Marc's wife say about Jean-Marc? *he is romantic*

7.5 Read the sentences and choose the appropriate picture, as in the example. There are more pictures than you need.

Example: J'adore le cyclisme.

1. Je vais envoyer une carte postale à ma tante.

2. J'adore jouer de la clarinette.

3. J'ai mal à la tête. Tu as quelque chose?

4. J'ai soif. Je peux boire un chocolat chaud?

5. Je vais souvent au cinéma et j'aime bien les comédies.

6. Mon sport préféré est l'athlétisme.

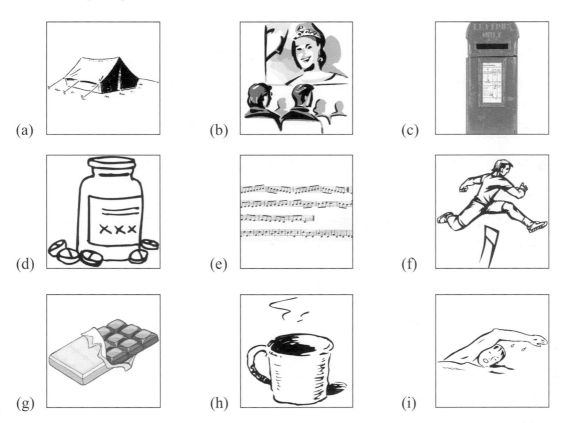

(a)   (b)   (c)

(d)   (e)   (f)

(g)   (h)   (i)

7.6   Match up the following types of programme with the programme titles.

1.   Les informations   (a)   Match of the Day

2.   Un dessin animé   (b)   Fireman Sam

3.   Un documentaire   (c)   The X Factor

4.   Un drame   (d)   News at Ten

5.   Une émission de musique   (e)   Neighbours

6.   Une émission de sport   (f)   Weather forecast

7.   Une émission pour les petits enfants (g)   The Simpsons

8.   La météo   (h)   Pride and Prejudice

9.   Une série australienne   (i)   Panorama

Writing

7.7   Write a sentence of between five and ten words for each picture below.

(a)   (b)   (c)

7.8   Write a letter of between 80 and 130 words to a French friend. You must mention at least four of the following points:

- Un cadeau d'anniversaire
- Des amis
- Un problème
- Une bonne idée
- Le sport

Test yourself

Before moving on to the next chapter, make sure you can answer the following questions. Answers, where relevant, are given at the back of the book.

1. Match up the French and English activities.

    1. Je joue avec mes copains.   (a) I have to do my homework.

    2. Je regarde les actualités.   (b) I want to play on the computer.

    3. J'aime lire les romans.   (c) I play with my friends.

    4. Je dois faire mes devoirs.   (d) I chat with my friends.

    5. Je veux jouer à l'ordinateur.   (e) I watch TV every evening.

    6. Je voudrais jouer aux cartes.   (f) I love cycling.

    7. J'aime lire les BDs.   (g) I like reading novels.

    8. J'adore faire du vélo.   (h) I am watching the news.

    9. Je bavarde avec mes amis.   (i) I would like to play cards.

    10. Je regarde la télé tous les soirs.   (j) I like reading comics.

2. Copy and complete with the correct French verb from the box below.

    (a) Je n'aime pas ....4........... en ville.

    (b) Elle déteste ....3.......... de la musique.

    (c) J'adore ....5.......... au netball.

    (d) J'aime ....1.......... du judo.

    (e) Il aime ....2.......... avec ses amis.

①	②	③	④	⑤
faire	bavarder	écouter	aller	jouer

Chapter 8: Life and work at school

In this chapter you will revise how to do the following:

1. Describe your school.
2. Describe the people in your school.
3. Talk about your school day.
4. Talk about school subjects.
5. Discuss what you like and dislike at school.
6. Understand classroom instructions.
7. Understand computer terminology.

The school day

les matières (f.)	subjects	l'éducation religieuse	religious education
le cours	lesson	la géo(graphie)	geography
la leçon	lesson	l'histoire (f.)	history
la récré(ation)	morning break	l'informatique (f.)	ICT
la pause-déjeuner	lunch break	la technologie	design technology
la réunion	assembly	les maths (f.)	maths
l'anglais (m.)	English	les sciences (f.)	science
l'art dramatique (m.)	drama	la biologie	biology
le français	French	la physique	physics
le grec	Greek	la chimie	chemistry
le latin	Latin	E.P.S.	P.E.
la cuisine	cooking	le sport	games

Comments

très bien	very good	difficile	difficult
fantastique	fantastic	dur	hard
intéressant	interesting	ennuyeux	boring
amusant	fun	formidable	great, fantastic
facile	easy		

A mon école il y a ...   In my school there is/are ...

le bureau	office
le centre sportif	sports centre
le couloir	corridor
le court de tennis	tennis court
le dortoir	dormitory
le gymnase	sports hall
l'internat (m.)	boarding house
le labo(ratoire) de sciences/de langues	science/language lab
le terrain de sport	sports field

la cour	playground
la grande salle	school hall
la piscine	swimming pool
la salle de classe	classroom
la salle d'informatique	computer room
la salle de musique	music room
la salle des professeurs	staff room
les bâtiments (m.)	buildings
les vestiaires (f.)	the changing rooms

Dans ma salle de classe il y a … | In my classroom there is/are …

le sac à dos	rucksack
le tableau blanc	whiteboard
le tableau électronique	interactive board
la chaise	chair

Dans mon sac il y a … | In my bag there is/are …

le compas	compass
la calculatrice	calculator
la trousse	pencil case
la règle	ruler
la gomme	eraser
le stylo	pen
le crayon	pencil
le livre	book
le cahier	exercise book
l'agenda (m.)	diary

Understanding classroom instructions

lève/levez la main!	put up your hand
lève-toi/levez-vous!	stand up
assieds-toi/asseyez-vous!	sit down
donne-moi …	give me …
ouvre la porte, s'il te plaît	open the door, please
ferme la fenètre	close the window
arrête/arrêtez!	stop
entre/entrez!	come in

8

Les gens

l'élève (m./f.)	pupil
le prof(esseur)*	teacher
le concierge	male caretaker
la concierge	female caretaker
le directeur	male headteacher
la directrice	female headteacher
l'instituteur (m.)	male primary school teacher
l'institutrice (f.)	female primary school teacher
sévère	strict
stricte	strict
gentil, gentille	kind

*French school children use the word 'prof' more frequently than 'professeur', particularly when speaking. The word professeur is masculine. If you are specifically talking about a female teacher, you can say 'la prof'.

Verbs

commencer	to begin
compter	to count
emprunter	to borrow
faire les devoirs	to do homework
passer un examen	to sit an exam
réussir	to succeed
réussir à un examen	to pass an exam

Useful phrases

Je suis en cinquième	I am in Year 8
Je suis externe	I'm a day pupil
Je suis interne	I'm a boarder
Je suis demi-pensionnaire	I am a half-boarder (eat lunch at school)
Je suis faible en biologie	I am weak at Biology
Je suis fort(e) en histoire	I am good at History
Ça s'écrit comment?	How do you spell that?
Excusez-moi	Excuse me
Je ne sais pas	I do not know
Ma matière préférée est …	My favourite subject is …
Chaque cours dure 45 minutes	Each lesson lasts 45 minutes
J'ai oublié	I have forgotten
Deux fois par semaine	Twice a week
Je n'ai pas de stylo	I don't have a pen
J'ai perdu …	I've lost …

Sample speaking passages

Read the sample passages aloud then say a few sentences about your school in the same way.

> Salut! Je m'appelle Jack et je vais à une école privée dans le sud de l'Angleterre. Il y a 300 élèves à l'école et elle se trouve à la campagne. Ma matière préférée est l'histoire car c'est intéressant et le professeur est assez stricte mais patient.

> Bonjour, je m'appelle Patricia et je vais au collège à Edimbourg. J'adore mon collège car je suis sportive et il y a beaucoup de choses à faire. Il y a des terrains de sport, des courts de tennis et un centre sportif. L'année prochaine ils vont construire une piscine couverte. C'est formidable!

> Je vais à l'école à pied parce qu'il y a trop de circulation. Je quitte la maison à sept heures quarante-cinq et j'entre dans ma salle de classe à huit heures cinq. Les cours commencent à neuf heures moins le quart après la réunion.

Sample questions

Try these sample questions for yourself. Answers are given at the back of the book.

Speaking

Oral discussions

8.1   (a) Décris une journée typique à l'école.
Describe a typical day at school.

(b) Combien de cours as-tu par jour?
How many lessons do you have each day?

(c) Les devoirs durent combien de temps?
How long does prep last?

(d) Quelles matières aimes-tu?
Which subjects do you like?

(e) Fais-moi une description de ton école.
Describe your school.

(f) Est-ce que tu aimes ton école? Pourquoi (pas)?
Do you like your school? Why (not)?

(g) Qu'est-ce que tu peux faire pendant la récréation?
What can you do during break?

8

(h) Qu'est-ce que tu aimes faire à l'école quand tu n'as pas de cours?
   What do you like to do at school when you do not have any lessons?

(i) Qu'est-ce que tu vas faire cet après-midi?
   What are you going to do this afternoon?

(j) Qu'est-ce que tu as fait hier à l'école?
   What did you do yesterday at school?

(k) Qu'est-ce que tu portes comme uniforme scolaire?
   What do you wear as school uniform?

Role-play practice

Look at the section on the Speaking paper (pages 9–12) for help with role plays.

8.2   You are at school in France with your penfriend. Try to say the following in French:

(a) Say that you do not have a pen.

(b) Ask your penfriend if he/she has a ruler.

(c) Ask the date.

(d) Say that the teacher speaks too fast.

(e) Ask what time the lesson ends.

(f) Say that the lessons are very long in France.

(g) Ask if there is a break soon.

8.3   You are at school in France with your penfriend. Try to say the following in French:

(a) Say that the school is very big.

(b) Ask how many pupils there are.

(c) Say that your school is smaller.

(d) Say that there are 80 boys and 55 girls.

(e) Ask at what time the first lesson begins.

(f) Say that lessons begin at 8.30 a.m. at your school.

8.4   You are at school in France and are talking to the teacher. Try to say the following in French:

(a) Ask the teacher if you can come in.

(b) Say that you are staying with your penfriend.

(c) Give your age.

(d) Say that you are here for one week.

(e) Ask if you have to do homework.

(f) Say that you do homework every day in England.

Sample questions

Try these sample questions for yourself. Answers are given at the back of the book.

Listening

8.5   Listen to Julie describe her school. For each sentence, choose the correct picture.

Exemple: Je me lève à sept heures = 2.

i.

ii.

iii.

(a) Je vais à l'école …

i.

ii.

iii.

(b) J'arrive à l'école à …

i.

ii.

iii.

(c) Ma matière préférée est …

i.

ii.

iii.

(d) Mercredi après-midi, nous avons un match de …

i.

ii.

iii.

(e) Ce soir, je dois …

i.

ii.

iii.

Track 8

8.6   Listen to the boy talking about his school and choose the correct answer as in the example.

Exemple: Mon école se trouve à Bordeaux.
Manchester, London, <u>Bordeaux</u>

(a)   It is a school for …   boys, girls, boys and girls

(b)   There are … pupils.   100, 170, 160

(c)   His favourite subject is …   PE, Biology, Physics

(d)   The teacher has …   long curly hair, short curly hair, short straight hair

(e)   He likes …   Art, Drama, Maths

Track 9

8.7   Listen to this boy and choose a picture for each subject he says, as in the example.

Exemple: J'adore jouer de la trompette.
Picture (1.)

1.

2.

3.

4.

5.

6.

Reading

8.8 Read the following passage, then copy and complete by filling in the gaps using the words in the box below. Each word can only be used once.

Mon école s'appelle Brockett Hall. C'est une école privée et .... Il y a environ deux cents .... de huit à .... ans et douze professeurs. Mon école est bien équipée. Par exemple, il y a un nouveau gymnase et la .... a été construite il y a dix-huit mois. Je ne suis pas très .... mais j'adore la lecture.

J'arrive à l'école à huit .... vingt et les cours .... quinze minutes plus tard. Il y a une récré à onze heures moins cinq et ça .... vingt-cinq minutes. Il y a beaucoup de .... pendant la pause-déjeuner. Pour les élèves qui aiment les sports, il y a des clubs comme le rugby et le netball mais, moi, j'aime jouer aux ....

Ma matière préférée, c'est l'histoire et je m'intéresse beaucoup à la deuxième guerre mondiale. J'ai horreur des sciences parce que le professeur n'est pas .... Je trouve les .... fatigantes et nous avons fait un .... hier matin.

patient	clubs	mixte	sportif	élèves	dure	heures	commencent
échecs	treize	bibliothèque	expériences	test			

Writing

8.9 Write a sentence of between five and ten words for each picture below.

(a)

(b)

8.10 Your French friend is coming to visit you and has asked you to send a brief description of life in an English school. Write 80–130 words and include four of the following points:

- Où se trouve ton école
- Tes matières préférées
- Le sport et les activités
- L'uniforme
- Les profs

L'informatique	Computing
cliquer sur …	to click on …
effacer	to delete
entrer	to enter, log on
répondre	to reply
sauvegarder	to save
sortir	to go out, log off
surfer sur Internet	to surf the internet
télécharger	to download
le clavier	keyboard
le courrier électronique	email
le document	document
le dossier	file
l'écran (m.)	screen
l'internet (m.)	internet
le mot de passe	password
l'ordinateur (m.)	computer
le site Internet/Web	website
l'imprimante (f.)	printer
la souris	mouse

Test yourself

Before moving on to the next chapter, make sure you can answer the following questions. Answers, where relevant, are given at the back of the book.

1. Read the descriptions of what happens in each room (on the left) and choose the correct classroom (on the right).

    Dans cette salle on étudie…

    (a) la langue et la littérature de la Grande Bretagne.

    (i)   la salle de musique

    (b) la biologie, la chimie et la physique.

    (ii) la salle d'anglais

    (c) les mélodies ou des chansons.

    (iii) la salle de géographie

    (d) les gens célèbres et les dates dans le passé.

    (iv) la salle d'histoire

    (e) les rivières, la campagne et la météo.

    (v)   le labo

2. Write down 10 things that you would find in a classroom. Check the list for your spellings.

Chapter 9: Holidays, weather, time and dates

In this chapter you will revise how to do the following:

1. Discuss the weather.
2. Talk about special days and events.
3. Discuss where you can stay on holiday.
4. Describe wherc you have been on holiday.
5. Talk about future holiday plans.

9.1 Weather, time and dates

Seasons

en automne	in autumn	au printemps	in spring
en hiver	in winter	en été	in summer

Weather adjectives

agréable	pleasant	froid*	cold
beau*	lovely, fine	humide	humid
brumeux	misty	mauvais*	bad
clair	clear	nuageux	cloudy
chaud*	hot	orageux	stormy
couvert	overcast	pluvieux	rainy
doux*	mild	sec	dry
frais	fresh	variable	variable

* Note these are used with the verb faire.

Examples

Il fait doux aujourd'hui.
It's mild today.

Il a fait chaud hier.
It was hot yesterday.

Le temps était agréable.
The weather was pleasant.

Le ciel est couvert.
The sky is overcast.

9

Weather nouns

l'arc en ciel (m.)	rainbow	la brume	mist
le ciel	sky	la chaleur	heat
un coup de tonnerre	a clap of thunder	des éclaircies (f. pl.)	sunny periods
un coup de vent	a gust of wind	la glace	ice
un éclair (m.)	a flash of lightning	la grêle	hail
le soleil	sun	la neige	snow
le tonnerre	thunder	la pluie	rain
le vent	wind	une tempête	a storm
le verglas	black ice	un orage	a storm

Weather phrases

Quel temps fait-il?	What is the weather like?
Il fait 30 degrés	It is 30 degrees
Il fait de la grêle	It is hailing
Il neige	It is snowing
Il pleut	It's raining
Il fait du tonnerre	It is thundering
Le soleil brille	The sun is shining
Il faisait beau	It was good weather
Il y avait de l'orage	It was stormy
Il neigeait	It was snowing
Il pleuvait	It was raining
Le soleil brillait	The sun was shining

Time nouns

le jour	day	le mois	month
quinze jours	a fortnight	le siècle	century
la journée	day (whole day long)	le lever du soleil	sunrise
toute la journée	the whole day	la coucher du soleil	sunset
le soir	evening	l'aube	dawn
la soirée	evening (all evening)		

Examples

J'ai passé quinze jours en Écosse.
I spent a fortnight in Scotland.

Elle a passé la soirée devant la télé.
She spent the evening in front of the TV.

Bonne journée!
Have a good day!

Bonne soirée!
Enjoy your evening!

When?

aujourd'hui	today
ce matin	this morning
cet après-midi	this afternoon
ce soir	this evening
hier	yesterday
hier soir	yesterday evening
avant-hier	the day before yesterday
la veille	the previous day
le weekend dernier	last weekend
la semaine dernière	last week
il y a trois mois	three months ago
pendant les vacances	in/during the holidays
demain	tomorrow
demain matin	tomorrow morning
après-demain	the day after tomorrow
le lendemain	the next day
l'an prochain (m.)	next year
dimanche prochain	next Sunday
la semaine prochaine	next week
à l'avenir	in the future
le premier avril	(on) the 1st of April
le deux février	(on) the 2nd of February

9

Special days

un jour férié	a bank holiday
un jour de fête	a day of celebration
l'anniversaire	birthday
une fête	a party
fêter	to celebrate
une fête religieuse	a religious festival
la Fête des Mères	Mothers' Day
la Fête des Pères	Fathers' Day
le Mardi Gras	Shrove Tuesday
le Jour de l'an	New Year's Day
Noël	Christmas
Pâques	Easter
le 14 juillet/la Fête Nationale	Bastille Day

Greetings

Bon anniversaire!	Happy birthday!
Bonne fête!	Enjoy your special day!
Joyeux Noël!	Happy Christmas!
Joyeuses Pâques!	Happy Easter!
Bonne année!	Happy New Year!
Bonnes vacances!	Have a good holiday!

Time and date phrases

Quelle heure est-il?	What time is it?
Il est trois heures	It is three o'clock
Il est trois heures cinq	It is five past three
Il est trois heures moins cinq	It is five to three
Il est trois heures et quart	It is quarter past three
Il est trois heures et demie	It is half past three
Il est trois heures moins le quart	It is quarter to three
Ça commence à quelle heure?	At what time does it begin?
À dix-huit heures	At 18.00
À minuit et demi	At half past 12 (midnight)
À midi et demi	At half past 12 (noon)
Quelle est la date aujourd'hui?	What is the date today?
C'est quand?	When is it?
C'est quand ton anniversaire?	When is your birthday?
C'est le cinq avril	It's the 5th of April

Tu es en avance	You are early
Tu es en retard	You are late
À tout à l'heure	See you soon
À ce soir	See you this evening
À bientôt	See you soon
Il se fait tard	It is getting late

Sample questions

Try these sample questions for yourself. Answers are given at the back of the book.

Speaking

Role-play practice

Look at the section on the Speaking paper (pages 9–12) for help with role plays.

9.1 You are on the phone to a French penfriend. Try to say the following in French:

(a) Ask what the weather is like there.

(b) Say it is warm but raining where you are.

(c) Ask your friend the date of his/her birthday.

(d) Ask your friend what they are going to do at Christmas.

(e) Say you love to go skiing in winter.

(f) Say you normally get up at 7.15.

(g) Say the telephone number is 01 42 35 78 56 (remember that French people always say telephone numbers in pairs).

Reading

9.2 Pick the good types of weather from the list below.

(a) Il fait beau

(b) Il neige

(c) Il ne fait pas chaud

(d) Il y a du brouillard

(e) Il gèle

(f) Il fait de l'orage

(g) Il fait mauvais

(h) Il pleut

(i) Il fait 30 degrés

9

9.3   Read the following advert and fill in the gaps in the questions below.

PISCINE EN PLEIN AIR
Heures d'ouverture
Du lundi au vendredi: de 10h à 12h30
                        de 14h à 17h
Le weekend: de 9h à 12h30
                        de 13h à 20h

TARIF
Entrée: **4 euros**
Enfants 5 à 13 ans: **3 euros**
Les moins de 5 ans: **gratuit**

Exemple: L'information est pour …

   (a) l'église

   (b) le cinéma

   (c) **la piscine**

1.   La piscine est ouverte à … le lundi.

   (a) 9 heures

   (b) 10 heures

   (c) 11 heures

2.   La piscine ferme à … le dimanche.

   (a) 6 heures

   (b) 8 heures

   (c) 10 heures

3.   Un garçon qui a treize ans paie …

   (a) 4 euros

   (b) 3 euros

   (c) 0 euros

4.   Une fille qui a quatre ans paie …

   (a) 4 euros

   (b) 3 euros

   (c) 0 euros

5. Un adulte paie …

(a) 4 euros

(b) 3 euros

(c) 0 euros

Writing

9.4 Write five to ten words in French on each of the following:

(a) Noël

(b) Le jour de l'an

(c) Pâques

(d) Le quatorze juillet

(e) La Fête des Mères

9

9.2 Describing holidays and holiday activities

Places to stay

l'hôtel (m.)	hotel	l'auberge (f.)	inn, small hotel
le gîte	rented cottage	le camping	campsite

At the hotel

le sèche-cheveux	hairdryer	la pension complète	full board
les bagages	luggage	la serviette	towel
la clef	key	la valise	suitcase
la demi-pension	half board	la vue sur la mer	sea view

Useful phrases

C'est …	It's …
au sous-sol	in the basement
au rez-de-chaussée	on the ground floor
au premier étage	on the first floor
au deuxième étage	on the second floor
au dessus de	above …
au dessous de	below …

At the campsite

le bloc sanitaire	wash block
la douche	shower
l'emplacement (m.)	pitch
la tente	tent
le camping-car	motorhome
le matelas pneumatique	airbed
le sac de couchage	sleeping bag
le feu	fire
le gaz	gas
l'allumette (f.)	match
l'ouvre-boîte (m.)	can opener
des plats à emporter	takeaway meals
l'eau non potable (f.)	non-drinking water
la pile	battery
la lampe de poche	torch

Examples

Est-ce que vous avez de la place?
Do you have any vacancies?

Est-ce que vous avez des chambres libres?
Do you have any rooms free?

À quel étage est la chambre?
On which floor is the bedroom?

Avez-vous de la place pour une tente pour quatre nuits?
Do you have space for a tent for four nights?

Je voudrais réserver un emplacement pour quatre personnes et une tente.
I would like to reserve a pitch for four people and a tent.

At the seaside

la mer	sea
le sable	sand
le rocher	rock
la falaise	cliff
la marée (basse/haute)	(low/high) tide
le bateau	boat
le phare	lighthouse
la crème solaire	suncream
le marchand de glaces	ice cream vendor
faire un barbecue	to have a barbecue
faire un pique-nique	to have a picnic

Countries and nationalities

L'Allemagne (f.)	Germany	allemand(e)	German
Les États-Unis (m.)	USA	américain(e)	American
L'Angleterre (f.)	England	anglais(e)	English
La Belgique	Belgium	belge	Belgian
Le Canada	Canada	canadien(ne)	Canadian
L'Écosse (f.)	Scotland	écossais(e)	Scottish
L'Espagne (f.)	Spain	espagnol(e)	Spanish
La France	France	français(e)	French
La Grande-Bretagne	Great Britain	britannique	British
L'Irlande (f.)	Ireland	irlandais(e)	Irish
Les Pays-Bas (m.)	Netherlands	Néerlandais(e)	Dutch
Le pays de Galles	Wales	gallois(e)	Welsh
La Suisse	Switzerland	suisse	Swiss

9

Useful phrases

Je suis en vacances	I am on holiday
Pendant les grandes vacances	During the summer holidays
Je suis allé(e) à Londres	I went to London
J'ai voyagé en voiture	I travelled by car
Je suis resté(e) à la maison	I stayed at home
J'ai passé une semaine en Écosse	I spent a week in Scotland
Je suis allé(e) à l'étranger	I went abroad

Positive opinions

J'ai aimé mon séjour parce que/qu' …	I liked my stay because …
C'était intéressant	It was interesting
Il faisait beau	There was good weather
J'ai fait beaucoup de choses	I did a lot of things
L'hôtel était énorme	The hotel was enormous
Il y avait une piscine en plein air	There was an outdoor swimming pool
La nourriture était délicieuse	The food was delicious

Negative opinions

Je n'ai pas aimé mon séjour parce que/qu' …	I didn't like my stay because …
C'était ennuyeux	It was boring
Il faisait froid	It was cold
Il faisait trop chaud	It was too hot
J'ai visité trop de musées	I visited too many museums
Il n'y avait pas de piscine	There was no swimming pool
L'hôtel était petit	The hotel was small

Sample speaking passages

Read the three passages aloud and note that each passage is in a different tense: the first is in the **present tense** as the person is saying what they **normally** do; the second is in the **past** talking about a holiday they have **spent** in Biarritz; the third is telling what they are **going** to be doing next year.

Now you make up a few sentences in the same way on the subject of your holidays.

Pendant les grandes vacances nous passons normalement une semaine au bord de la mer. J'adore aller à la plage. Je nage et je joue au foot avec mes frères.

J'ai aimé mon séjour à Biarritz parce que l'hôtel était énorme avec une piscine magnifique et un très bon restaurant. Aussi, l'hôtel était à cent mètres de la plage. Le dernier jour j'ai nagé dans la mer avant le petit déjeuner et, après avoir mangé, je suis allé en ville acheter des cadeaux pour mes amis.

L'année prochaine je vais au Canada. Ça va être formidable! Nous allons rester chez mes cousins qui habitent à Vancouver. Je vais faire du kayak et de la voile et nous allons faire des randonnées dans la forêt.

Sample questions

Try these sample questions for yourself. Answers are given at the back of the book.

Speaking

Oral discussions

9.5 (a) Qu'est-ce que tu aimes faire pendant les grandes vacances?
What do you like to do during the summer holidays?

(b) Décris une journée typique pendant les vacances.
Describe a typical day during the holidays.

(c) Qu'est-ce que tu aimes faire quand il fait chaud?
What do you like to do when it is hot?

(d) Où es-tu allé(e) en vacances l'année dernière?
Where did you go on holiday last year?

(e) Décris-moi un peu ces vacances.
Tell me a little about this holiday.

9

Role-play practice

Look at the section on the Speaking paper (pages 9–12) for help with role plays.

9.6   You are on the beach and meet a French child. Try to say the following in French:

(a)   Introduce yourself.

(b)   Say that it is very hot today.

(c)   Ask where he/she lives.

(d)   Ask if the weather is always good.

(e)   Say that you are here for two weeks

(f)   Say that you spend your holidays here every year.

9.7   You are at a campsite. Try to say the following in French:

(a)   Ask for a pitch.

(b)   Say that you have one tent.

(c)   Say that there are five people in your family.

(d)   Say that you would like to stay for four nights.

(e)   Ask where the wash block is.

(f)   Ask if there is a swimming pool.

9.8   You are at a hotel. Try to say the following in French:

(a)   Ask if they have any rooms free.

(b)   Say that it is for two adults and three children.

(c)   Ask how much it is.

(d)   Ask if the room has a shower.

(e)   Ask if it is possible to eat in the hotel now.

(f)   Ask if there is a restaurant nearby.

Listening

9.9 Match each description you hear with the correct event below.

1. Le Jour de l'an

2. L'Armistice 1918

3. La Fête Nationale

4. Pâques

Reading

9.10 Read the following passage and answer the questions below in English.

Cette année nous avons passé une semaine dans un petit camping au bord de la mer. Nous avons loué une tente parce que, l'année dernière, on a eu un accident avec notre tente quand il faisait trop de vent. J'ai monté la tente avec Papa pendant l'après-midi et Maman est allée au magasin avec mes deux petites sœurs. Il faisait très chaud donc Maman a acheté des glaces pour tout le monde et nous nous sommes assis sous un arbre. C'était un grand emplacement donc il y avait beaucoup d'espace pour notre voiture et les cinq vélos.

J'étais un peu fatigué, alors j'ai cherché un matelas pneumatique et je me suis reposé pendant un quart d'heure pendant que Papa finissait tout. Après dix minutes il a décidé d'aller au café pour acheter des plats à emporter. Il voulait préparer un barbecue mais c'était interdit parce que l'emplacement se trouvait à côté d'un bois.

(a) How long did they spend on holiday?

(b) What happened last year?

(c) How many people are there in the family?

(d) What did Mum buy?

(e) Why is a mattress mentioned?

(f) What did Dad want to do?

(g) Why could he not do it?

9.11   Read the following passage and answer the questions below in French.

> La Tour Eiffel a été construite en 1889 pour L'Exposition Universelle de Paris, qui a célébré le centenaire de la Révolution française. Il y avait un concours et les plans de Monsieur Gustave Eiffel ont été choisis. Après deux ans, on a fini la construction et la Tour Eiffel est restée l'édifice le plus haut du monde jusqu'à 1930. Elle mesure trois cents mètres et il y a trois niveaux. Il y a eu une pétition signée pour protester contre sa construction mais, actuellement, c'est une des attractions les plus célèbres du monde entier. Il y a un restaurant, un bar et une boutique. C'est aussi très utile avec son antenne pour la radio et la télévision française.

(a)   Quand est-ce que la Tour Eiffel a été construite?

(b)   Pourquoi est-ce que la Tour Eiffel a été construite?

(c)   Combien de mètres mesure la tour?

(d)   Pourquoi est-ce qu'il y a eu une pétition signée?

(e)   Pourquoi la Tour est-elle utile?

Writing

9.12   Write a sentence of between five and ten words for each picture below.

(a)

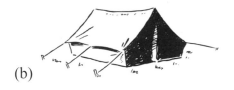
(b)

9.13   You are writing to a French friend about a special day. Write a letter of 80–130 words. You must mention at least four of the following points:

● Le départ en bus

● La plage

● Le repas

● Les activités

● Le soir

9.14 You are spending a week at a seaside resort and each day you fill in your diary. You can mention the weather, where you have been, what you have been doing, who you have met, what you have eaten etc. Write five to ten words for each daily entry.

Lundi:

Mardi:

Mercredi:

Jeudi:

Vendredi:

Samedi:

Dimanche:

Test yourself

Before moving on to the next chapter, make sure you can answer the following questions. Answers, where relevant, are given at the back of the book.

1.   How many types of weather can you say in French? Try to write them down and check your spellings from the list.

2.   Do you know the French for Christmas, New Year, Easter, Shrove Tuesday, Bastille Day?

3.   C'était comment?

Work out which of these opinions are positive and which are negative:

génial	bizarre	excellent	bruyant	extra
super	bien	trop long	formidable	bon marché
nul	incroyable	trop court	intéressant	trop cher
désastreux	fantastique	chouette	affreux	ennuyeux
tranquille	stressant	confortable	cool	

4.   Which of these activities are often done on the beach?

(a) Je mange une glace au chocolat.

(b) Je joue avec un ballon.

(c) Je fais du shopping.

(d) Je fais mes devoirs.

(e) Je passe l'aspirateur.

(f) Je me bronze.

9

Chapter 10: Health and fitness

In this chapter you will revise the following:

1. Parts of the body.
2. How to talk about your health.
3. How to explain health problems to the doctor or chemist.

Parts of the body

la tête	head	le pied	foot
la gorge	throat	le genou	knee
la main	hand	le bras	arm
la jambe	leg	le ventre	stomach
l'oreille (f.)	ear	le dos	back
la dent	tooth	l'oeil (m.)	eye
l'épaule (f.)	shoulder	les yeux	eyes

Qu'est-ce qui ne va pas?   What's the matter?

J'ai mal à la tête	I have a headache
J'ai mal à l'oreille	I have earache
J'ai mal au dos	I have a sore back
J'ai mal aux yeux	My eyes hurt

Health

le médecin	doctor	le paracétamol	paracetamol
l'infirmier (m.)	male nurse	l'aspirine (f.)	aspirin
l'infirmière (f.)	female nurse	le pansement	dressing, bandage
la maladie	illness	le sparadrap	sticking plaster
un rhume	a cold	la pharmacie	pharmacy
la grippe	flu	le pharmacien	chemist
le médicament	medicine	le tube de crème solaire	tube of suncream
le comprimé	tablet, pill	un coup de soleil	sunstroke

Verbs

avoir besoin de	to need
avoir chaud	to feel hot
avoir faim	to be hungry
avoir froid	to feel cold
avoir le mal de mer	to be seasick
avoir soif	to be thirsty
casser	to break
être en forme	to be fit
être malade	to be ill
fumer	to smoke
grossir	to gain weight
maigrir	to lose weight
mourir	to die
prendre rendez-vous	to make an appointment
prendre un coup de soleil	to get sunstroke
se blesser	to injure oneself
se faire mal	to hurt oneself
vomir	to vomit

Useful phrases

J'ai froid	I'm cold
J'ai chaud	I'm hot
Je suis malade	I am ill
Ça ne va pas	I'm not well
Je dois rester au lit	I must stay in bed
Je me suis cassé la jambe	I have broken my leg
Elle va téléphoner au médecin*	She is going to phone the doctor
Bonjour, Docteur*	Good morning, Doctor

*Note that the normal word for 'doctor' is 'médecin' but you address him as 'Docteur'.

Writing practice!

Write an email to a French friend explaining that you are at home today because you are unwell. Explain what the problem is, whether you have been to the doctor, how you are feeling now and what you are planning to do tomorrow.

Sample questions

Try these sample questions for yourself. Answers are given at the back of the book.

Speaking

Role-play practice

Look at the section on the Speaking paper (pages 9–12) for help with role plays.

10.1 You are at the chemist's. Try to say the following in French:

    (a) Say that you are ill.

    (b) Say that you have a headache.

    (c) Say that you are very hot.

    (d) Ask if you can telephone the doctor.

    (e) Ask the name of the doctor.

    (f) Say that you are staying with your French friend.

10.2 You are not feeling well. Try to say the following in French:

    (a) Say that you have earache.

    (b) Say that you are not able to sleep.

    (c) Say that you are not hungry.

    (d) Ask where the chemist's is.

    (e) Ask if the chemist's is open today.

    (f) Ask for a paracetamol.

Reading

10.3 Read the following problems and match the name of the person to one of the correct statements (a)–(e) below.

> Je dois porter des lunettes mais je ne veux pas les porter parce que les autres élèves dans ma classe se moquent de moi. Je ne peux pas bien voir si je ne les porte pas et j'ai mal à la tête.

Anne

> Tous les matins je me lave soigneusement mais je suis adolescent et des boutons se sont formés sur tout mon visage. Qu'est-ce que je peux faire?

Paul

> J'ai voulu changer la couleur de mes cheveux mais, la semaine dernière, j'ai commencé à perdre mes cheveux. Je ne veux pas me cacher de mes amis donc qu'est-ce que je peux faire?

Martine

> J'adore aller à la plage avec mes copines. Nous jouons au volley et j'adore me bronzer. Est-ce que le bronzage présente des dangers?

Cathérine

> Mon frère est très sportif et il joue toujours au basket avec ses amis. Il dit que je dois y jouer aussi mais je ne suis pas en forme et je suis assez gros. Je veux maigrir mais je ne sais pas comment.

Marc

(a) I worry about sunbathing.

(b) I want to get thinner.

(c) I do not want to wear my glasses.

(d) I worry about dyeing my hair.

(e) I would like advice about my spots.

10

Writing

10.4 Write a sentence of between five and ten words for each picture, as in the example.

Example: Je joue au squash pour garder la forme.

(a)   (b)

Test yourself

Now you have completed this chapter, make sure you can answer the following questions. Answers are given at the back of the book.

1. Read the following sentences and decide which part of the body each is describing from the list below.

    (a) J'en ai besoin pour manger un sandwich.

    (b) J'en ai besoin pour courir.

    (c) J'en ai besoin pour jouer de la guitare.

    (d) J'en ai besoin pour lire un roman.

    (e) J'en ai besoin pour me promener.

les mains	la tête	le genou	les jambes	les cheveux
le nez	la bouche	les yeux	les oreilles	les pieds

2. Which of the following would you find in a hospital?

    (a) Un comprimé   (f) Un médecin

    (b) Un chien   (g) Du sparadrap

    (c) Un maillot de rugby   (h) Une voiture

    (d) Un infirmier   (i) Une boucherie

    (e) Un autobus   (j) Une aspirine

Appendix A – Transcripts for the listening passages

Listening

*   *   *

Exercise 4.5: Listen to Marc talking about himself and the members of his family and give at least two details for each one.

Salut! Moi, je m'appelle Marc et j'ai onze ans. J'ai les cheveux assez longs et marron et les yeux bleus.

J'ai une grande famille: il y a mes deux parents et trois frères. Ma mère s'appelle Françoise et elle est petite et mince. Elle a les cheveux roux, courts et frisés.

Mon père s'appelle Philippe et il a quarante ans. Il est grand et un petit peu gros. Il a les yeux bleus et il est chauve.

Mes trois frères s'appellent Matthieu, Luc et Jean. Matthieu a quinze ans et il est très sportif. Il est musclé et bronzé et il adore jouer au rugby.

Luc a treize ans et il est très intelligent. Il a les cheveux marron comme moi et il adore le rock.

Jean a cinq ans. Il a les cheveux blonds et courts, il est assez petit et très mignon. Il a des tâches de rousseur.

*   *   *

Exercise 4.6: Listen to the man talking about his family and pick the correct answer, as in the example.

Exemple: Je m'appelle Jean-Marc et j'ai cinquante ans.

(a)   Il y a cinq personnes dans notre famille.

(b)   J'ai deux fils et une fille.

(c)   Ma femme a les cheveux longs et raides.

(d)   Je suis professeur.

(e)   Je quitte la maison à huit heures moins vingt-cinq.

Track 3

Exercise 5.4: Listen to the following passage and pick the phrases you hear from the list below.

Tous les jours je me réveille à sept heures et, dix minutes plus tard, je me douche. Je m'habille et puis je fais mon lit. À sept heures trente-cinq je descends pour prendre mon petit déjeuner. Normalement, c'est Papa qui prépare le petit déjeuner et moi je mets la table. Quand nous avons fini, Maman débarrasse la table et je donne à manger au chien.

✳ ✳ ✳

Track 4

Exercise 6.4: Listen to these people and choose the place where they should go.

(a) Je viens d'écrire une lettre à ma tante mais je n'ai pas de timbres.

(b) Vous avez un plan de la ville, s'il vous plaît?

(c) Maman, il n'y a plus de jambon pour mon sandwich.

(d) Papa, j'ai très mal à la tête. Tu as des aspirines?

(e) Nous allons à la messe demain matin à dix heures.

✳ ✳ ✳

Track 5

Exercise 6.5: Listen to the conversation and choose TRUE or FALSE for each sentence below, as in the example.

Le reporter:	Bonjour Anne. Tu as quel âge?
Anne:	J'ai treize ans.
Le reporter:	Est-ce que tu reçois de l'argent de poche?
Anne:	Oui mais je dois aider mes parents à la maison.
Le reporter:	Qu'est-ce que tu fais pour aider tes parents?
Anne:	Chaque matin je dois ranger ma chambre avant d'aller à l'école.
Le reporter:	Et qu'est-ce que tu fais le week-end?
Anne:	Je nettoie la maison avec Maman et je fais la vaisselle.
Le reporter:	Tu fais quelque chose avec ton père?
Anne:	Oui, mon père est handicapé. Nous aimons jouer aux échecs pendant que Maman fait les courses.
Le reporter:	Qu'est-ce que tu fais avec tes amis?
Anne:	S'il fait beau, je vais en ville avec mon amie Laura. Nous aimons acheter des vêtements et, quelquefois, nous allons au parc bavarder avec nos amis.

Exercise 7.3: Listen to this telephone conversation and answer the questions below in English.

Track 6

Marc	Salut Anne. Tu veux aller au cinéma mercredi soir? Il y a un super film de science-fiction que j'ai envie de voir.
Anne:	Mercredi soir? Non, je ne peux pas. Je dois aller chez ma grand-mère car c'est son anniversaire. En plus, je déteste les films de science-fiction.
Marc:	La semaine prochaine alors? On pourrait aller au stade de rugby voir le match. Qu'en penses-tu?
Anne:	Bonne idée! On se retrouve où? Devant le stade?
Marc:	Je préfère en face de la bibliothèque parce qu'il y a moins de monde.
Anne:	Pas de problème. Et on se retrouve à quelle heure?
Marc:	Vers treize heures trente?
Anne:	Fantastique. Rendez-vous samedi prochain, treize heures trente en face de la bibliothèque. À la semaine prochaine.

* * *

Exercise 8.5: Listen to Julie describe her school. For each sentence, choose the correct picture.

Track 7

Exemple: Je me lève à sept heures.

(a)   Je vais à l'école en car.

(b)   J'arrive à l'école à huit heures dix.

(c)   J'adore les ordinateurs.

(d)   Mon sport préféré est le hockey mais mercredi après-midi, nous avons un match de tennis.

(e)   Ce soir, mes parents vont chez ma grand-mère mais je dois rester chez moi faire mes devoirs.

* * *

Exercise 8.6: Listen to the boy talking about his school and choose the correct answer as in the example.

Track 8

Exemple: Mon école se trouve à Bordeaux.

(a)   C'est une école mixte.

(b)   Il y a cent soixante-dix élèves.

(c)   Ma matière préférée, c'est la physique.

(d) Le professeur de physique est petit avec les cheveux courts et frisés.

(e) Je ne suis pas sportif mais j'aime l'art dramatique.

*   *   *

Exercise 8.7: Listen to this boy and choose a picture for each thing he says, as in the example.

Track 9 **Exemple:** J'adore jouer de la trompette.

(a) Vite, Marc. Le court est libre en ce moment. Tu as les raquettes?

(b) Je voudrais être acteur.

(c) Tu aimes les poèmes?

(d) Je ne comprends pas les fractions.

(e) J'adore faire les expériences dans le labo.

*   *   *

Exercise 9.9: Match each description you hear with the correct event below.

Track 10 (a) C'est une fête d'origine chrétienne pour célébrer la résurrection de Jésus. Pour la plupart des Français c'est une fête non-religieuse où la famille se réunit pour manger un gigot d'agneau et des oeufs en chocolat.

(b) C'est une fête qui marque le début de la nouvelle année. On rend visite à sa famille et à ses amis et souvent on envoie des cartes pour leur dire bonne année.

(c) C'est un jour qui symbolise la fin de la monarchie française et le début de la République. Le quatorze juillet se fête dans toute la France avec de la musique, de la danse, de la chanson et des feux d'artifice.

(d) C'est l'anniversaire de la fin du combat entre l'Allemagne et les Alliés après les quatre ans de la première guerre mondiale.

150

Grammar section answers

1.   (a)   J'*aime* jouer au squash.
           I like playing squash.

      (b)   Tu *regardes* le film ce soir?
           Are you watching the film this evening?

      (c)   Il *travaille* dans le jardin.
           He is working in the garden.

      (d)   Elle *mange* un sandwich au jambon.
           She is eating a ham sandwich.

      (e)   Nous *préférons* la robe rose.
           We prefer the pink dress.

      (f)   Vous *écoutez* la radio?
           Are you listening/Do you listen to the radio?

      (g)   Ils *entrent* dans la salle de classe.
           They are going into the classroom.

      (h)   Elles *habitent* dans un bungalow.
           They live in a bungalow.

2.   (a)   Je *choisis* une glace.
           I am choosing an ice cream.

      (b)   Tu *finis* tes devoirs?
           Are you finishing your homework?

      (c)   Il *punit* les élèves méchants.
           He is punishing the naughty pupils.

      (d)   Elle *réussit* tout le temps.
           She always succeeds.

      (e)   Nous *grossissons*.
           We are putting on weight.

      (f)   Vous *maigrissez*?
           Are you losing weight?

      (g)   Ils *finissent* les exercices dans la salle de classe.
           The are finishing the exercises in the classroom.

      (h)   Elles *choisissent* de nouveaux vêtements.
           They are choosing some new clothes.

3.   (a)   Je *tonds* la pelouse.
           I am mowing the lawn.

      (b)   Tu *entends* les enfants?
           Do you hear the children?

(c) Il *descend* l'escalier.
He is going downstairs/down the stairs.

(d) Elle *répond* aux questions.
She is replying to the questions.

(e) Nous *attendons* une réponse à notre message électronique.
We are waiting for a reply to our email.

(f) Vous *vendez* des glaces?
Do you sell ice creams?

(g) Ils *vendent* des légumes au marché.
They sell vegetables at the market.

(h) Elles *descendent* de l'autobus devant l'église.
They are getting off the bus in front of the church.

4. (a) Je *m'habille* dans ma chambre.
I get dressed in my bedroom.

(b) Tu *te lèves* à sept heures trente.
You get up at half past seven.

(c) Il *se rase* devant un miroir.
He shaves in front of a mirror.

(d) Elle *se brosse* les dents dans la salle de bains.
She brushes her teeth in the bathroom.

(e) Nous *nous réveillons* très tôt chaque matin.
We wake up very early every morning.

(f) Vous *vous réveillez* à quelle heure?
At what time do you wake up?

(g) Ils *se coiffent* après le petit déjeuner.
They do their hair after breakfast.

(h) Elles *s'intéressent* à l'histoire.
They are interested in history.

5. (a) Elle a tort.

(b) Pierre a peur des vaches.

(c) Tu as très chaud.

(d) Ma mère a raison.

(e) J'ai besoin d'un stylo.

6. (a) Je *suis* très contente.
I am very glad/content/pleased.

(b) Tu *as* quel âge?
How old are you?

(c) Il *met* une chemise bleue.
He is putting on a blue shirt.

(d) Elle *ouvre* la porte.
She is opening the door.

(e) Nous *écrivons* une lettre à notre oncle.
We are writing a letter to our uncle.

(f) Vous *voulez* quelque chose à boire?
Do you want something to drink?

(g) Ils *vont* au cinéma ce soir.
They are going to the cinema this evening.

(h) Elles *viennent* chez nous à dix-neuf heures.
They are coming to our house at 7 p.m.

7. (a) Je veux sortir.

(b) Tu aimes jouer au tennis?

(c) Nous pouvons aller au cinéma.

(d) Je voudrais habiter en France.

(e) Je déteste faire les courses.

(f) Elle doit rester à la maison.

8. (a) Elle va arriver cet après-midi.

(b) Ils vont jouer sur l'ordinateur.

(c) Il va s'habiller.

(d) Nous allons choisir un livre.

(e) Est-ce que tu vas retourner l'année prochaine?

(f) Vous allez chanter ce soir.

(g) Paul va danser avec Anne.

(h) Elles vont jouer aux cartes après le déjeuner.

9. (a) *J'ai fini* mes devoirs.

(b) *J'ai attendu* l'autobus.

(c) *Il a joué* aux cartes.

(d) *Elle a choisi* de nouvelles chaussures.

(e) *Nous avons regardé* la télé.

(f) *Vous avez entendu* le bruit.

(g) *Ils ont répondu* aux questions.

(h) *Elles ont écouté* de la musique.

10. (a) J'ai bu de la limonade.

    (b) Elle a conduit la voiture.

    (c) Il a fait ses devoirs.

    (d) Tu as écrit une lettre.

    (e) Vous avez lu un magazine.

    (f) Nous avons couru très vite.

    (g) Ils ont mis les vêtements dans leur chambre.

    (h) Elles ont eu un accident.

11. (a) Je suis parti(e) à trois heures.

    (b) Elle est sortie à six heures quinze/et quart.

    (c) Il est arrivé à l'hôpital avec ses parents.

    (d) Nous sommes descendu(e)s à la cuisine.

    (e) Vous êtes allé(e)s au cinéma hier soir?

    (f) Ils sont venus au café avec leurs amis.

    (g) Elles sont entrées dans le salon.

    (h) Tu es rentré à quatre heures moins dix.

12. (a) Nous avons fini.

    (b) Elle est partie.

    (c) Nous sommes venus.

    (d) Elle a joué.

    (e) Les garcons sont tombés.

13. (a) Elle s'est habillée dans sa chambre.

    (b) Pierre s'est cassé la jambe.

    (c) Il s'est lavé dans la salle de bains.

    (d) Nous nous sommes couché(e)s après le film.

    (e) Elles se sont disputées.

    (f) Ils se sont promenés dans le parc.

    (g) Tu t'es levé(e) très tôt.

    (h) Vous vous êtes sauvé(e)s l'année dernière.

    (i) Nous nous sommes assis(es) sous un arbre.

14. (a) Il écoutait de la musique.

    (b) Nous regardions la télé.

    (c) Elles travaillaient dans une ferme.

    (d) Ils jouaient au cricket.

    (e) Tu lisais une lettre dans le bureau.

(f) Vous écoutiez la radio?

(g) Il faisait froid.

(h) Elle était professeur.

15. (a) I have not eaten anything.

(b) She is not happy/pleased.

(c) We did not see the lions.

(d) He never drinks lemonade.

(e) We do not have any more bananas.

16. (a) We did not see anyone.

(b) Nobody understands the passage.

(c) I saw neither Pierre nor Louise.

(d) It is only on Saturday evenings that we go to the cinema.

(e) He only goes to his favourite café.

17. (a) un

(b) la

(c) des

(d) de l'

(e) du

(f) une

(g) des

(h) aux

(i) à la

(j) à l'

(k) du

(l) aux

18. (a) rouge

(b) délicieuse

(c) bonne

(d) gentille

(e) petite… brune

(f) intelligents

(g) vieille

19. (a) un grand cheval noir

(b) une petite soeur

(c) les cheveux longs

(d) chère Julie

(e) un T-shirt cher

(f) une jolie fille

(g) des chaussures brunes

(h) un professeur intelligent

20. (a) Notre maison

(b) Votre tante

(c) Sa mère

(d) Ses chats

(e) Nos enfants

(f) Ta chambre

(g) Leur école

(h) Ma grand-mère

21. (a) à gauche de la boucherie

(b) chez Simon

(c) derrière le marché

(d) pendant le match

(e) en face de l'église

(f) sous la table

(g) sur la commode

(h) à côté de la banque

(i) avec mes amis

(j) dans la salle de classe

22. (a) sans moi

(b) pour lui

(c) derrière toi

(d) avant nous

(e) avec elle

(f) chez eux/chez elles

Sample question answers

Chapter 4: Family, friends and pets

4.1   The following are examples of possible answers only.

   (a)   Bonjour Monsieur, bonjour Madame.

   (b)   Comment allez-vous?

   (c)   Je vais bien merci.

   (d)   Je vais vous présenter ma famille.

   (e)   Et voici mon chien.

4.2   The following are examples of possible answers only.

   (a)   Salut Julie.

   (b)   Ça va bien merci, et toi?

   (c)   Rendez-vous où?

   (d)   Non, je préfère devant la gare.

   (e)   A demain.

   (f)   Bonne nuit.

4.3   The following are examples of possible answers only.

   (a)   Je m'appelle Gertrude et j'ai treize ans. Je suis assez grande et mince et j'ai les
         cheveux noirs. Je suis bavarde mais très polie.

   (b)   Il y a cinq personnes dans ma famille: mon père, ma mère, mes deux frères et moi.
         Mes frères s'appellent Mark et Peter et je suis la plus petite. J'ai aussi mon petit
         chien Bob!

   (c)   J'ai deux frères. Ils s'appellent Mark et Peter et je suis la plus petite.

   (d)   Mon père est medécin/homme d'affaires/agent de police.
         Ma mère est secrétaire/femme d'affaires/institutrice.

   (e)   Oui, j'ai un petit chien noir qui s'appelle Bob et cinq cochons d'Inde. Je promène Bob
         dans la forêt avec ma mère.
         Non. Je n'ai pas d'animaux domestiques mais je voudrais une tortue.

   (f)   Mon meilleur ami (*masculine*) s'appelle Henry et il a douze ans. Il est très gros, petit
         et laid. Il a les cheveux roux et courts. Il aime bien jouer aux échecs et il est très
         bavard.

         Ma meilleure amie (*feminine*) s'appelle Jenny et elle a treize ans. Elle est grande et
         mince et elle a les cheveux longs, blonds et raides. Elle est très jolie mais elle n'est
         pas très intelligente.

4.4 (a) Bonjour. Je m'appelle Marc/Sophie.

(b) J'habite avec mes parents.

(c) Je suis fils unique/fille unique.

(d) Mon père est grand, mince et très sportif.

(e) Ma mère est dentiste.

(f) Tu as des animaux domestiques?

4.5 In the grid below are all the details about each person. You need to have at least two from each list.

Person	Details
Marc	11 years old; quite long brown hair; blue eyes
Mother	called Françoise; small and thin; red hair; short curly hair
Father	called Philippe; 40 years old; tall and a bit fat; blue eyes; bald
Matthieu	15 years old; very sporty; muscular; tanned; loves playing rugby
Luc	13 years old; very intelligent; brown hair; loves rock music
Jean	5 years old; short blond hair; cute; quite short; has freckles

4.6 (a) Five

(b) Two boys and a girl

(c) Long straight (hair)

(d) Teacher

(e) 7.35

4.7 (a) héros

(b) célèbre

(c) laid

(d) je sens mauvais

(e) chauve

(f) ma nouvelle femme

(g) une ogresse

(h) la plus belle du monde

(i) un gilet

(j) sale

4.8 (a) On a farm in the countryside

    (b) Teach him new tricks

    (c) A horse

    (d) Chases anyone who goes into the field.

    (e) He was late for school so he took a short cut.

    (f) A pear tree

    (g) By throwing a pear for Rex to chase

4.9 The following are examples of possible answers only.

    (a) Voici ma mère avec ma petite soeur qui s'appelle Claire.

    (b) Nous avons un grand chien noir et blanc.

Chapter 5: House, home, daily routine and chores

5.1 The following are examples of possible answers only.

    (a) Ma maison est grande et jolie.

    (b) C'est à la campagne et elle se trouve dans un petit village près de Sherborne.

    (c) Il y a cinq chambres, deux salles de bains, un salon, une salle à manger et une cuisine.

    (d) Dans ma chambre il y a un petit lit, une armoire, une commode et une assez grande table. Sur la table il y a un ordinateur, des livres et un miroir.

    (e) Il y a un jardin derrière/devant/autour de ma maison. Il y a beaucoup de fleurs et des arbres. J'aime bien les pommiers et les sapins.

    (f) Ma maison idéale est très grande avec une piscine en plein air et un jacuzzi. Je voudrais aussi un gymnase et une salle de jeux pour mon frère, ma sœur et moi.

    (g) Il y a mon père, ma mère, mes deux frères Philip et Mark, ma sœur Elizabeth et moi.

    (h) Oui, j'aime bien ma maison./Non, je ne l'aime pas beaucoup.

    (i) Je joue sur l'ordinateur dans ma chambre et je joue au foot dans le jardin avec mon frère/ma sœur. Le weekend, je joue aux échecs avec mon père ou je bavarde avec ma mère.

    (j) Le samedi matin je lave la voiture pour mon père et, après ça, je promène le chien dans le bois derrière la maison. Je fais la vaisselle, je mets la table, je range ma chambre et je passe l'aspirateur.

5.2 (a) J'aime bien ma chambre.

    (b) Ma chambre en Angleterre est très petite.

    (c) J'habite dans une ferme.

    (d) Tu te lèves à quelle heure?

    (e) Est-ce que je peux prendre un bain?

    (f) Je voudrais me coucher.

5.3 (a) J'habite dans une maison.

(b) J'habite dans les environs de Londres./J'habite dans la banlieue de Londres.

(c) Il y a quatre chambres dans ma maison.

(d) Il y a un jardin derrière ma maison.

(e) Je lave les voitures.

(f) Quelquefois je fais du babysitting.

5.4 You should have picked the following phrases:

(a) I wake up

(c) I get dressed

(d) I make my bed

(e) I go downstairs

(g) I lay the table

(j) I feed the dog

5.5 (a) TRUE

(b) FALSE

(c) FALSE

(d) FALSE

(e) TRUE

(f) FALSE

5.6 You should have picked the following:

(d) Sa sœur ne fait rien.

(e) Maman est toujours fâchée s'il ne range pas ses vêtements.

(f) Eric doit ramasser ses vêtements.

(h) Eric fait ses devoirs avant le dîner.

(i) Papa aide Eric dans la cuisine après le dîner.

5.7 The following are examples of possible answers only.

(a) Nous habitons une grande maison à la campagne.

(b) Je fais mes devoirs tous les soirs avant le dîner.

5.8 The following is an example of a possible answer only.

Cher Jean-Paul,

Comment vas-tu? J'espère que tu vas venir bientôt chez moi.

J'habite une assez grande maison près du centre-ville. J'aime beaucoup habiter ici parce qu'il y a beaucoup de magasins tout près et je peux promener le chien dans le parc en face.

Nous avons une très grande cuisine et un salon au rez-de-chaussée et au premier étage il y a quatre chambres. Ma chambre est petite mais je l'aime bien. Derrière la maison il y a un jardin où j'aime lire quand il fait beau.

Normalement je me lève à sept heures et quart. Je prends mon petit déjeuner vers huit heures moins le quart – normalement un jus de fruit et des céréales – et je quitte la maison à huit heures vingt. Normalement je vais à l'école à pied car elle n'est pas loin de chez moi.

L'école finit à quatre heures et je rentre tout de suite. Je prends mon goûter et puis je promène le chien. Je fais mes devoirs avant le dîner puis je lis ou je regarde la télé. Je me couche à neuf heures et demie mais le weekend je me couche beaucoup plus tard.

A bientôt,

John

Chapter 6: In town, travel and transport, food and drink

6.1   The following are examples of possible answers only.

(a)   Il y a beaucoup de choses à faire près de chez moi. Ma sœur aime faire les magasins en ville mais, moi, j'adore faire du bowling et puis aller au cinéma.

(b)   Non, je n'aime pas faire du shopping. Je préfère aller à la patinoire./Oui, je vais en ville chaque weekend avec mes amies et j'achète de nouveaux vêtements.

(c)   J'achète mes bonbons à la petite confiserie sur la place principale en ville.

6.2   (a)   Je voudrais changer de l'argent.

(b)   J'ai des livres sterling.

(c)   Je voudrais deux cents euros.

(d)   J'ai mon passeport.

(e)   Est-ce que la banque est ouverte le samedi?

(f)   À quelle heure ouvre la banque lundi?

6.3   (a)   Où se trouve le supermarché?

(b)   Il s'appelle Carrefour.

(c)   C'est loin d'ici?

(d)   C'est le grand bâtiment à droite?

(e)   Est-ce qu'il y a une Poste près d'ici?

(f)   Est-ce qu'il y a une boîte aux lettres près d'ici?

6.4   (a)   Post office

(b)   Tourist office

(c)   Delicatessen

(d)   Chemist

(e)   Church

6.5 (a) TRUE

(b) FALSE

(c) TRUE

(d) FALSE

(e) FALSE

6.6

(a) La pharmacie	**La banque**	(b) La librairie	**L'épicerie**	(c) La poissonnerie
La rue				
(d) Le supermarché	**La Poste**	(e) La boulangerie	(f) Le cinéma	(g) La pâtisserie

6.7 The following are examples of possible answers only.

(a) Je préfère voyager en voiture car c'est confortable.

(b) Je préfère voyager en avion car c'est plus rapide.

(c) À mon avis, le moyen de transport le plus confortable est l'avion.

6.8 (a) Je voudrais un billet deuxième classe pour Paris, s'il vous plaît.

(b) Non, un aller-retour.

(c) À quelle heure est-ce que le prochain train part?

(d) De quel quai part le train?

(e) À quelle heure est-ce que le train arrive à Paris?

(f) Est-ce que je dois changer?

6.9 (a) Je voudrais aller à Lille demain.

(b) Est-ce qu'il y a un train vers midi?

(c) Est-ce qu'il arrive à Lille avant quatorze heures?

(d) C'est très rapide.

(e) Est-ce que c'est direct?

(f) Je voudrais un aller-simple, s'il vous plaît.

6.10 (a) Je voyage en bus.

(b) Le bus est en retard.

(c) Le bus va arriver à onze heures.

(d) On va arriver devant l'église.

(e) Le billet coûte dix euros.

(f) À bientôt.

6.11 The following is an example of a possible answer only.

Chère Anne,

Nous sommes bien arrivés à Versailles.

Nous avons pris le train de Reading à Londres, puis le métro à la Gare de St Pancras. Notre Eurostar est parti à dix-sept heures et nous sommes arrivés deux heures plus tard à Paris. Le voyage sous la Manche est très rapide. Je dois dire que le train est le moyen de transport que je préfère. Le train est confortable, il y a un buffet, et il n'y a pas de délai quand il fait du brouillard.

Quand nous sommes descendus du train à la Gare du Nord, nous avons attendu nos amis qui devaient venir nous chercher, mais ils ne sont pas venus. Où étaient-ils? Finalement ils nous ont téléphoné pour nous dire que leur voiture était tombée en panne. Nous avons dû prendre un taxi à Versailles et cela nous a coûté cher! Papa n'était pas content.

J'adore rester chez nos amis à Versailles. La maman est anglaise et son mari est français. Ils ont une fille qui a le même âge que moi et un petit chien adorable.

A Versailles il y a beaucoup de choses à voir. La ville est très jolie et il y a le château magnifique avec ses beaux jardins. Nous allons visiter le château cet après-midi.

Bisous,
Marie

6.12 The following are examples of possible answers only.

(a) Je prends le petit déjeuner à sept heures trente.

(b) J'adore les bananes.

(c) Je préfère le jambon mais j'aime aussi l'agneau.

(d) J'aime les sandwichs au fromage.

(e) Normalement je bois de l'eau minérale mais, quelquefois, je bois du jus d'orange.

6.13 (a) Je voudrais une table près de la fenêtre, s'il vous plaît.

(b) Une limonade et un jus de pomme, s'il vous plaît.

(c) Je voudrais du melon, s'il vous plaît.

(d) Je prends le poulet-frites.

(e) Qu'est-ce que vous avez comme dessert?

(f) Deux glaces à la vanille, s'il vous plaît.

6.14 (a) Je voudrais une table pour cinq personnes, s'il vous plaît.

(b) Pas près de la porte.

(c) La table est sale.

(d) Mes parents voudraient une bouteille de vin rouge.

(e) Je voudrais un verre de limonade.

(f) Je n'ai pas de serviette.

6.15

	Le Bosquet	Chez Pierre	Le Petit Lapin
Chips			✓
Duck	✓		
Rice		✓	
Egg			✓
Goat's cheese	✓		
Apple	✓		

6.16 The following are examples of possible answers only.

(a) Je vais au marché tous les samedis avec Maman.

(b) L'été dernier nous avons voyagé à Paris en train.

(c) J'aime voyager en avion parce que c'est très rapide.

6.17 The following is an example of a possible answer only.

Chère Madeleine,

Nous avons passé une journée formidable à Edimbourg le weekend dernier pour fêter mon anniversaire. Nous habitons à la campagne alors c'est toujours un plaisir de visiter la ville.

Je me suis levée de bonne heure et j'ai pris mon petit déjeuner en vitesse: un chocolat chaud, des toasts et de la confiture d'oranges. Est-ce que tu aimes la confiture d'oranges?

A huit heures et demie nous sommes partis en voiture à Edimbourg. Il faisait beau et le paysage était très joli. Les petits agneaux dans les champs avaient l'air contents! Nous sommes arrivés une heure plus tard et nous avons trouvé un parking au centre-ville.

Il y avait beaucoup de monde, surtout dans la vieille ville. J'ai vu des touristes américains, japonais, allemands, et même français! J'ai voulu visiter le château mais nous ne sommes pas entrés parce que Papa a dit que c'était un peu cher. Alors nous sommes allés au musée des jouets – c'est très amusant!

A midi nous avons déjeuné dans un petit restaurant où j'ai pris un steak-frites délicieux. Comme dessert il y avait un grand choix de glaces. On a vraiment bien mangé!

Nous avons quitté Edimbourg à cinq heures. J'ai dormi dans la voiture! C'était une journée fantastique.

Ecris-moi bientôt,
Amitiés,
Laura

Chapter 7: Free time

7.1 The following are examples of possible answers only.

    (a) Je joue au rugby/foot/golf/netball/tennis.
           Je fais de la natation./Je nage.
           Je fais de l'équitation./Je fais du cheval.
           Je collectionne des timbres.
           Je fais du vélo/VTT.
           Je fais de la voile/planche à voile.

    (b) Je joue au rugby/foot/golf/netball/tennis.
           Je fais de la natation./Je nage.
           Je fais de l'équitation./Je fais du cheval.

    (c) Je préfère jouer au squash.

    (d) Je préfère la musique pop/la musique classique/le jazz/le hard. C'est cool et j'aime bien Britney/Mozart etc.

    (e) Oui, je joue de la trompette depuis deux ans.

    (f) Je vais au cinéma avec mes copains deux fois par mois.

    (g) Quand je suis avec mes copains je vais au parc et je fais du skate.

    (h) Le weekend prochain je vais aller chez mon oncle et ma tante car c'est l'anniversaire de mon cousin Max.

    (i) J'aime jouer au foot dans le jardin.
           J'adore lire mes livres dans ma chambre.

    (j) Je me suis levé à dix heures.
           J'ai joué au foot dans le jardin avec mon ami Fred.

    (k) Je fais du shopping en ville avec ma copine Marie.
           Je mange beaucoup de fast-food devant la télé.

7.2 (a) Tu veux aller au cinéma?

    (b) Il y a un film d'aventures à quinze heures.

    (c) C'est un film avec Tom Cruise.

    (d) Rendez-vous devant le cinéma.

    (e) Rendez-vous à quatorze heures trente.

    (f) Tu veux aller en ville après?

7.3 (a) Wednesday evening.

    (b) She has to go to her grandmother's house as it is her birthday and she does not like science fiction films.

    (c) A rugby match.

    (d) Opposite the library.

    (e) There are fewer people.

    (f) About 1.30 p.m.

7.4 (a) From time to time.

(b) A film called *Maman, j'ai raté l'avion* (*Home Alone*).

(c) There are too many people./He prefers staying at home with his family and dogs./He does not like popcorn.

(d) Action films.

(e) Gérard Depardieu.

(f) He fell asleep.

(g) A magician.

(h) Ugly.

(i) He is very romantic.

7.5 1. (c)

2. (e)

3. (d)

4. (h)

5. (b)

6. (f)

7.6 1. Les informations   (d) News at Ten

2. Un dessin animé   (g) The Simpsons

3. Un documentaire   (i) Panorama

4. Un drame   (h) Pride and Prejudice

5. Une émission de musique   (c) The X Factor

6. Une émission de sport   (a) Match of the Day

7. Une émission pour les petits enfants (b) Fireman Sam

8. La météo   (f) Weather forecast

9. Une série australienne   (e) Neighbours

7.7 The following are examples of possible answers only.

(a) Hier j'ai joué au squash avec mon ami Henri.

(b) Je joue de la trompette depuis trois ans.

(c) Le weekend dernier ma famille et moi sommes allés au théâtre.

7.8 The following is an example of a possible answer only.

Cher Philippe,

Hier, c'était l'anniversaire de mon ami Stephen. Je suis allé en ville tôt pour lui acheter un cadeau. Malheureusement, j'ai oublié mon porte-monnaie et j'ai dû retourner à la maison! En tout cas, je n'avais pas beaucoup d'argent, alors mon père m'a donné quelques euros. J'ai visité de nombreux magasins, mais je n'ai pas trouvé un bon cadeau pour mon ami. J'étais très vexé! Mais quand je passais devant le stade j'ai eu une bonne ideé. Je suis allé au guichet et j'ai acheté deux billets pour le match. Notre équipe a gagné; c'était formidable!

Amitiés,
Paul

Chapter 8: Life and work at school

8.1 The following are examples of possible answers only.

(a) J'arrive à l'école à huit heures et quart et nous avons l'appel à huit heures et demie. Le premier cours commence à neuf heures et il y a trois cours avant la récré qui est à onze heures. Je prends mon déjeuner à la cantine à une heure moins dix et, après ça, il y a une autre récré. Je fais du sport pendant l'après-midi. En été je joue au cricket et je fais de l'athétisme. Je rentre à la maison à cinq heures, je prends mon goûter puis je fais mes devoirs.

(b) Nous avons huit cours par jour.

(c) Les devoirs durent une heure.

(d) J'aime l'histoire et la géo parce qu'elles sont intéressantes et je les trouve faciles mais je préfère les maths car le prof est très gentil et je suis fort en maths.

(e) Mon école est assez grande et elle se trouve à Londres. C'est une école mixte avec deux cents élèves. À l'école il y a beaucoup de salles de classe, un gymnase, une cantine, une bibliothèque, des terrains de sport et des courts de tennis. Malheureusement, il n'y a pas de piscine.

(f) J'aime bien mon école car les profs sont gentils et il y a beaucoup de choses à faire./ Je n'aime pas mon école car les cours sont ennuyeux.

(g) Pendant la récréation je joue au foot/je bavarde avec mes amis/je lis/je joue au tennis.

(h) Je joue au foot./Je bavarde avec mes amis./Je lis./Je joue au tennis.

(i) Cet après-midi je vais jouer au cricket.

(j) Hier c'était dimanche donc je suis resté(e) chez moi avec ma famille.

(k) Comme uniforme je porte un pantalon noir, une chemise bleue, un pull gris et une cravate bleue.

8.2 (a) Je n'ai pas de stylo.

(b) Tu as une règle?

(c) Quelle est la date?

(d) Le professeur parle trop vite.

(e) À quelle heure finit le cours?

(f) Les cours sont très longues en France.

(g) Est-ce qu'il y a une récréation bientôt?

8.3 (a) L'école est très grande.

(b) Il y a combien d'élèves?

(c) Mon école est plus petite.

(d) Il y a quatre-vingts garçons et cinquante-cinq filles.

(e) À quelle heure commence le premier cours?

(f) Les cours commencent à huit heures et demie à mon école.

8.4 (a) Je peux entrer?

(b) Je reste chez mon correspondant/ma correspondante.

(c) J'ai treize ans.

(d) Je suis ici pour une semaine.

(e) Est-ce que je dois faire les devoirs?

(f) On fait les devoirs tous les jours en Angleterre.

8.5 (a) iii. Coach

(b) ii. 8.10

(c) iii. ICT/Computer Studies

(d) ii. Tennis

(e) i. Do homework

8.6 (a) Boys and girls

(b) 170

(c) Physics

(d) Short curly hair

(e) Drama

8.7 (a) 4. Tennis

(b) 3. Drama

(c) 5. English

(d) 2. Maths

(e) 6. Science

8.8 Mon école s'appelle Brockett Hall. C'est une école privée et **mixte**. Il y a environ deux cents **élèves** de huit à **treize** ans et douze professeurs. Mon école est bien équipée. Par exemple, il y a un nouveau gymnase et la **bibliothèque** a été construite il y a dix-huit mois. Je ne suis pas très **sportif** mais j'adore la lecture.

J'arrive à l'école à huit **heures** vingt et les cours **commencent** quinze minutes plus tard. Il y a une récré à onze heures moins cinq et ça **dure** vingt-cinq minutes. Il y a beaucoup de **clubs** pendant la pause-déjeuner. Pour les élèves qui aiment les sports, il y a des clubs comme le rugby et le netball mais, moi, j'aime jouer aux **échecs**.

Ma matière préférée, c'est l'histoire et je m'intéresse beaucoup à la deuxième guerre mondiale. J'ai horreur des sciences parce que le professeur n'est pas **patient**. Je trouve les **expériences** fatigantes et nous avons fait un **test** hier matin.

8.9 The following are examples of possible answers only.

(a) Ma matière préférée est l'histoire parce que le professeur est drôle.

(b) J'adore la musique mais je ne chante pas bien.

8.10 The following is an example of a possible answer only.

Chère Anne,

Merci beaucoup pour ta lettre. Je vais te parler de mon école.

J'habite assez près de l'école alors j'y vais à pied normalement. Les cours commencent à huit heures et demie. Nous avons trois cours avant la récré, puis deux cours avant la pause-déjeuner. Ma matière préférée est le français parce que c'est intéressant et je suis assez forte en langues, mais je n'aime pas les maths. Tous les profs sont gentils, sauf Madame Jones, notre prof de sciences. Elle est très stricte.

Deux fois par semaine nous faisons du sport. J'adore ça, surtout en été quand nous jouons au tennis. En hiver nous jouons au hockey. Tu aimes la natation? A l'école nous avons une piscine magnifique alors n'oublie pas ton maillot de bain!

Comme uniforme je porte une jupe verte avec une chemise jaune et un pull vert. Je déteste mon uniforme. En France on ne porte pas d'uniforme – tu as de la chance!

Et toi, comment est ton école? Ecris-moi bientôt.

Amicalement,
Sophie

Chapter 9: Holidays, weather, time and dates

9.1   The following are examples of possible answers only.

(a)   Quel temps fait-il, là-bas?

(b)   Ici il fait chaud, mais il pleut.

(c)   Quelle est la date de ton anniversaire?

(d)   Qu'est que tu vas faire à Noël?

(e)   J'adore faire du ski en hiver.

(f)   Je me lève normalement à sept heures et quart.

(g)   Le numéro est zéro-un, quarante-deux, trente-cinq, soixante-dix-huit, cinquante-six.

9.2   You should have picked the following:

(a) Il fait beau

(i) Il fait 30 degrés

9.3   (b)   10 heures

(b)   8 heures

(b)   3 euros

(c)   0 euros

(a)   4 euros

9.4   The following are examples of possible answers only.

(a)   Normalement nous passons Noël assez tranquillement à la maison.

(b)   Le premier janvier, je visite mes tantes et mes oncles.

(c)   J'aime beaucoup le chocolat, alors j'aime bien Pâques!

(d)   Le quatorze juillet nous avons regardé les feux d'artifice.

(e)   Je vais offrir des fleurs à maman pour la Fête des Mères.

9.5   The following are examples of possible answers only.

(a)   Pendant les grandes vacances j'aime aller à la plage avec mes copains.
J'aime aller chez mon oncle Harry qui habite à Londres.

(b)   Je me lève à dix heures et je me douche. Je prends mon petit déjeuner devant la télé et puis je joue sur l'ordinateur jusqu'à midi. Après mon déjeuner je vais en ville ou à la plage avec mes copains et je m'amuse bien.

(c)   Je vais à la plage avec mes copains ou je joue au foot dans le parc.

(d)   Je suis allé(e) en France/Écosse/Allemagne
Je suis allé(e) au Japon/Canada.
Je suis allé(e) aux États-Unis.

(e)   Je suis allé(e) en France avec ma famille et nous avons loué un gîte dans le sud. Nous sommes allé(e)s à la plage chaque jour et nous avons nagé.

9.6 (a) Bonjour. Je m'appelle John.

    (b) Il fait très chaud aujourd'hui.

    (c) Où habites-tu?

    (d) Est-ce qu'il fait toujours beau?

    (e) Je suis ici pour deux semaines.

    (f) Je passe mes vacances ici chaque année.

9.7 (a) Je voudrais un emplacement, s'il vous plaît.

    (b) Nous avons une tente.

    (c) Il y a cinq personnes dans ma famille.

    (d) Nous voulons rester quatre nuits.

    (e) Où se trouve le bloc sanitaire?

    (f) Est-ce qu'il y a une piscine?

9.8 (a) Vous avez des chambres libres?

    (b) C'est pour deux adultes et trois enfants.

    (c) C'est combien?

    (d) Est-ce qu'il y a une douche dans la chambre?

    (e) Est-ce qu'on peut manger à l'hôtel maintenant?

    (f) Est-ce qu'il y a un restaurant près d'ici?

9.9 (a) 4. Pâques

    (b) 1. Le Jour de l'an

    (c) 3. La Fête Nationale

    (d) 2. L'Armistice 1918

9.10 (a) A week

    (b) There was an accident with the tent because it was too windy.

    (c) Five

    (d) Ice creams for everyone

    (e) He was tired so laid down on it for 15 minutes.

    (f) Prepare a barbecue

    (g) The pitch is next to a wood so barbecues are forbidden.

9.11 (a) La Tour Eiffel a été construite en 1889.

    (b) La Tour Eiffel a été construite pour L'Exposition Universelle de Paris.

    (c) Elle mesure trois cents (300) mètres.

    (d) Il y a eu une pétition signée pour protester contre sa construction.

    (e) Parce qu'il y a une antenne pour la radio et la télévision française.

9.12 The following are examples of possible answers only.

(a) Pendant les vacances de Noël j'ai fait du ski.

(b) Nous allons faire du camping au bord de la mer.

9.13 The following is an example of a possible answer only.

Salut Marc,

Nous nous amusons ici dans notre gîte. Je vais te raconter notre journée à la plage hier.

Après le petit déjeuner nous avons pris le bus pour aller à une petite plage à trois kilomètres du gîte et nous avons passé toute la matinée dans la mer. A midi nous sommes allés au restaurant où nous avons mangé des fruits de mer délicieux et des glaces au chocolat. L'après-midi nous avons joué avec le grand ballon rouge que Papa a acheté dans un petit kiosque. Il y avait beaucoup de touristes sur la plage et malheureusement, quand mon frère a lancé le ballon, il est tombé sur une vieille dame qui dormait au soleil. Elle était très fâchée! Mes parents aussi. Le soir, quand nous sommes rentrés au gîte nous avons dû lire des magazines parce que Papa a confisqué le ballon!

Ecris-moi bientôt,
Charles

9.14 The following are examples of possible answers only.

Lundi:	Je suis arrivé à l'hôtel et je suis très fatigué.
Mardi:	Aujourd'hui nous avons fait du shopping et j'ai acheté un nouveau T-shirt.
Mercredi:	Nous sommes allés à l'aquarium ce matin car il pleuvait.
Jeudi:	Le soleil brillait donc Papa a loué un petit bateau.
Vendredi:	Encore du soleil alors ma soeur a bronzé sur le balcon.
Samedi:	J'ai joué au foot dans le parc avec des touristes italiens.
Dimanche:	Nous avons fait nos valises parce que nous allons partir demain matin.

Chapter 10: Health and fitness

10.1 (a) Je suis malade.

(b) J'ai mal à la tête.

(c) J'ai très chaud.

(d) Est-ce que je peux téléphoner au médecin?

(e) Comment s'appelle le médecin?

(f) Je reste chez mon ami(e) français(e).

10.2 (a) J'ai mal à l'oreille.

(b) Je ne peux pas dormir.

(c) Je n'ai pas faim.

(d) Où se trouve la pharmacie?

(e) Est-ce que la pharmacie est ouverte aujourd'hui?

(f) Puis-je avoir un paracétamol?

10.3 (a) Cathérine

(b) Marc

(c) Anne

(d) Martine

(e) Paul

10.4 The following are examples of possible answers only.

(a) Je vais me coucher parce que j'ai mal à la tête.

(b) Quand maman a mal à la tête elle prend de l'aspirine.

Test yourself answers

Chapter 4: Family, friends and pets

1. The following are examples of possible answers only.

    (a) Salut!

    (b) Enchanté (or) Bonjour Monsieur, bonjour Madame.

    (c) Je te présente ma sœur.

    (d) Ça va?

    (e) Comment allez-vous, madame?

    (f) Rendez-vous à la piscine.

    (g) Au revoir, à samedi.

2. (a) *J'a* les cheveux noirs, courts et frisés.

    (b) *J'ai* les yeux verts.

    (c) *Je suis* très mince.

    (d) *J'ai* trois frères.

    (e) *Je suis* assez courageux.

    (f) *Je suis* grosse et petite.

    (g) *J'ai* onze ans.

    (h) *Je suis* sympa.

    (i) *Je suis* méchant mais poli.

    (j) *J'ai* un chien et trois poissons rouges.

Chapter 5: House, home, daily routine and chores

1. (a) J' *habite* à Londres.

    (b) Ma chambre *est* en face de la chambre de ma sœur.

    (c) Mon frère *met/débarasse* la table.

    (d) Je me *brosse* les dents dans la salle de bains.

Chapter 6: In town, travel and transport, food and drink

1. 1. Antiques   (l)

    2. Bakery   (a)

    3. Beware of the dog (x2)   (d, n)

    4. Cake shop   (h)

    5. 24 hours   (f)

    6. Danger of death (x2)   (e, m)

7. Exit   (b)

8. Fires forbidden   (g)

9. Kitchen   (i)

10. Stop   (c)

11. Toilets (x2)   (k, o)

12. Veterinary surgeon   (j)

2. (a) à vélo

    (b) en voiture

    (c) en bateau

    (d) en train

    (e) en avion

Chapter 7: Free time

1. 1. Je joue avec mes copains.   (c) I play with my friends.

    2. Je regarde les actualités.   (h) I am watching the news.

    3. J'aime lire des romans.   (g) I like reading novels.

    4. Je dois faire mes devoirs.   (a) I have to do my homework.

    5. Je veux jouer à l'ordinateur.   (b) I want to play on the computer.

    6. Je voudrais jouer aux cartes.   (i) I would like to play cards.

    7. J'aime lire les BDs.   (j) I like reading comics.

    8. J'adore faire du vélo.   (f) I love cycling.

    9. Je bavarde avec mes amis.   (d) I chat with my friends.

    10. Je regarde la télé tous les soirs. (e) I watch TV every evening.

2. (a) Je n'aime pas *aller* en ville.

    (b) Elle déteste *écouter* de la musique.

    (c) J'adore *jouer* au netball.

    (d) J'aime *faire* du judo.

    (e) Il aime *bavarder* avec ses amis.

Chapter 8: Life and work at school

1. (a) la langue et la littérature de la Grande Bretagne   (ii) la salle d'anglais

    (b) la biologie, la chimie et la physique   (v)   le labo

    (c) les mélodies ou des chansons   (i)   la salle de musique

    (d) les gens célèbres et les dates dans le passé   (iv) la salle d'histoire

    (e) les rivières, la campagne et la météo   (iii) la salle de géographie

Chapter 9: Holidays, weather, time and dates

3.

Positive	Negative
génial	bizarre
excellent	bruyant
extra	nul
incroyable	désastreux
super	stressant
bien	trop cher
formidable	trop long
bon marché	ennuyeux
intéressant	trop court
fantastique	affreux
chouette	
tranquille	
confortable	
cool	

4. Activities normally done on the beach:

(a) Je mange une glace au chocolat.

(b) Je joue avec un ballon.

(f) Je me bronze.

Chapter 10: Health and fitness

1. (a) La bouche

(b) Les jambes

(c) Les mains

(d) Les yeux

(e) Les pieds

2. (a) Un comprimé

(d) Un infirmier

(f) Un médecin

(g) Du sparadrap

(j) Une aspirine

Galore Park
PRACTICE EXERCISES

   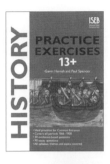 

 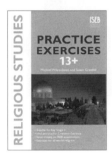  

- Many titles endorsed by the Independent Schools Examination Board

- Perfect for 11+, 13+ and scholarship entrance exam preparation

- Packed full of practice exercises so pupils are fully prepared for their exam

- Enables pupils to identify gaps in knowledge for focused revision

- Familiarisation with the exam format to avoid nasty surprises in the exam room!

- Answers provided to enable pupils to check their progress

- Separate books for three Latin levels

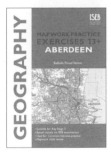

ISEB
Independent Schools
Examinations Board

For more information please visit our website:
www.galorepark.co.uk

Galore Park
VOCABULARY BOOKS

GALORE PARK

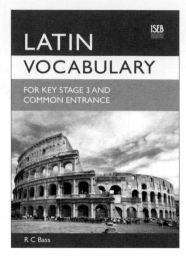

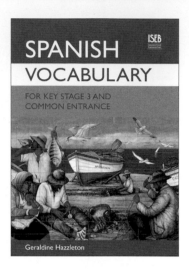

- Endorsed by the Independent Schools Examination Board

- Invaluable for pupils preparing for Key Stage 3 and 13+ Common Entrance exams

- Organised by topic so pupils can focus their revision

- Words arranged alphabetically, then in sections for ease of learning

- Useful phrases to enable pupils to understand usage

- Available for French, Spanish and Latin

ISEB
Independent Schools
Examinations Board

For more information please visit our website:
www.galorepark.co.uk